D1364924

WHY I FLY FISH

Passionate Anglers on the Pastime's Appeal
& How It Has Shaped Their Lives

Chris Santella

STEWART, TABORI & CHANG

NEW YORK

TABLE OF CONTENTS

ACKNOWLEDGMENTS

This book would not have been possible without the generous assistance of the passionate anglers who shared their time and insights to explore how the sport of fly fishing can impact us. To these folks, I offer the most heartfelt thanks. I would especially like to thank **Mac McKeever** and **Robert Tomes**, who both offered encouragement and made many introductions on my behalf. I also wish to acknowledge the fine efforts of my agent **Stephanie Kip Rostan**; my editor **Jennifer Levesque**; designers **Henk van Assen, Loide Marwanga**, and **Marcela de la Vega**; and copyeditor **Magdalena Schmidt** who all helped bring the book into being. I've had the good fortune over the last thirty years to make many fine fishing friends. This list includes **Peter Marra, Ken Matsumoto, Jeff Sang, Joe Runyon, Mark Harrison, Peter Gyerko, Tim Purvis, Geoff Roach, Kenton Quist, Mike Marcus, Nelson Mathews, Kevin Wright, John Smith, David Moscowitz, Ken Helm, Chris Conaty, Bryce Tedford, Darrell Hanks, Hamp Byerly, Mac McKeever, Robert Tomes, Conway Bowman,** and **Kirk Deeter,** among many others. I look forward to many more days on the river with these friends and friends to come. I also extend kudos to **Sloan Morris, Keith Carlson,** and **Doug Mateer,** who've helped put fly fishing to music in our band, Catch & Release. Finally, I want to extend a special thanks to my wife, **Deidre**, and my daughters, **Cassidy** and **Annabel**, who've humored my absence on far too many occasions so I could explore what fly fishing means to me…and to my parents, **Andy** and **Tina Santella**, who are not anglers, but who always encouraged me to pursue my passions.

INTRODUCTION

THERE'S AN APHORISM that goes something like "God does not subtract from the allotted span of men's lives the hours spent in fishing." The quote has been attributed to a number of sources, including Muhammad, the eighth-century BCE philosopher Piscius, and an Assyrian tablet dating from 2000 BCE. Whether you ascribe the sentiment to divine or more earthly sources, it suggests that fishing has long had a certain spiritual component that transcends being merely another way of putting food on the table.

I would like to think that man and woman might get a few extra hours in their allotted lifespan for time spent *fly fishing*.

People constantly ask me what the appeal of fly fishing is. My neighbors, my children's friends and their parents, and strangers in airports gawk at my expanse of gear bags and want to know: Is it the grace of casting? Is it because flies work better than lures? Did I start because of *A River Runs Through It* (what people in the industry simply call "the movie")? I have trouble answering the question succinctly. But the question so frequently posed to me got me thinking and got me asking my angling companions about their motivations for taking up the long rod. I was astounded by the range of responses, and by how deeply the sport seemed to resonate for so many of its practitioners…and how at times it seemed to inform other aspects of their lives.

The desire to record and share some of these fly fishers' observations on their motivations and satisfactions in fly fishing was the impetus for *Why I Fly Fish*. As a freelance writer who has covered fly fishing for the last decade, I've been fortunate enough to get to know many people around the fly-fishing field, from journalists (like John Gierach and Kirk Deeter) to television personalities (like Flip Pallot and

Conway Bowman) to ardent conservationists (like Craig Mathews and Chris Wood) to guides (like April Vokey). In addition to gleaning their perspectives, I thought it would be interesting to get a view on the sport from people who've made their marks in other areas of endeavor, but who have a passion for the sport: figures from the business world (Bill Ford and Donald Trump Jr.), the entertainment field (Henry Winkler and James Williamson), professional sports (Nick Price), the world of letters (Carl Hiaasen), and the political realm (Robert Rubin and Senator Mike Enzi).

The combined perspectives of these fly anglers and their stories will hopefully shed a bit more light on a passion that will drive its practitioners to rouse themselves well before sunrise and return home well after dark with nothing for the frying pan; endure driving rain, near-freezing temperatures, insect bites, and body bruises (from hard-fighting fish) in the name of amusement; squander their eyesight trying to tie on flies that are dwarfed by your pinky nail; and tell nonstop stories that will glaze over the eyes of all but the most devoted fellow anglers.

Fly fishers will understand.

And fly fishers in the making may find good reason to give the sport a try!

THE PERSPECTIVES

CONWAY BOWMAN
It's about the journey

IF YOU'VE EVER BEEN INCLINED to scan your cable offerings in search of a fly-fishing infusion, chances are good that you've come upon an intense Californian with piercing blue eyes—namely, Conway Bowman. Conway has played host on several fishing shows, most recently *Fly Fishing the World* on the Sportsman Channel. Most would agree that Conway's ongoing quest for mako sharks in the waters off San Diego, California, has catapulted him to fly-rod celebrity, a status that has all the gravitas in the nonfishing world of being, in his words, "the world's tallest midget." Although sharks may have placed an exclamation point on Conway's fly-fishing career, smaller prey provided an early defining moment.

"I grew up in the San Diego area," Conway began, "and my dad was a schoolteacher. In the summer months, he'd go to Idaho to fly fish, and he'd take me along. One day when I was eight, we were fishing on the Henry's Fork. My dad had waded out toward the middle of the river, as there were lots of trout rising out there. I was stuck on the bank with my fly rod, as I was too small to wade. A man with a moustache and a white ten-gallon hat walked up. To an eight year old, he looked like the Marlboro Man. 'How's it going?' he asked. 'Are you catching anything?' I was a little dejected and said 'Nope.' He said, 'Okay, tie this ant on and cast down the bank.' 'Right next to the bank?' I asked, and he said 'Yep.' I tied the ant on and on the third or fourth cast, I caught a sixteen-inch rainbow. The stranger—who turned out to be

Mike Lawson (who started Henry's Fork Anglers)—netted the fish and showed it off to my dad, who came to the bank at that moment with a gigantic trout of his own. That was the first time I ever saw a fish come up and take the fly. I can still see the take, still hear Mike telling my dad about the fish I'd caught."

Summers were fruitful on the fly-fishing front for Conway, but the rest of the year was a bit lacking. There just aren't many trout streams in greater San Diego. After spending a few winters fishing for bass in local reservoirs, Conway noticed a fairly large body of water to the west and realized that it might hold promise…and that sharks were among the most plentiful sport fish off the coast of San Diego. "I bought a seventeen-foot aluminum skiff with a twenty-five horse tiller–controlled motor and a compass and handheld radio," Conway explained. "I would run that skiff so far out that I couldn't see land! There were some dicey times when the fog would roll in and I was ten miles out to sea but I made it back and look at those times as not stupid moves, but valued learning experiences. The first time I went fly fishing for sharks, I conned one of my buddies, Mike Seim, to venture out with me. We set a chum slick (a stew of yellowtail carcasses, seasoned with a few table-spoons of menhaden oil), and by the end of the day we had landed twenty-five blue sharks ranging from four to eight feet long. At that point I realized that I was onto something fly-rodding for sharks. But it took me two years to catch my first mako on the fly." (Sadly Mike, who went on to become a well-respected guide in Montana, died in 2011.)

Suffice it to say, fly fishing for mako sharks is not a dainty game. In addition to the telephone pole of a fly rod, reels are outfitted with eight hundred yards of backing, a stainless steel leader, and foot-long blaze orange flies tied on 8/o hooks. On an aver-age day, Bowman will motor a few miles offshore to a spot where a current moves through. The current will broadcast a chum slick, which draws sharks close because of its olfactory appeal. Sometimes it takes a while for a shark to appear, sometimes its appearance is almost instantaneous. "When you're fishing for makos, the sharks are hunting you, not the other way around," Conway said. "They're not shy; when they turn on, they're like heat-seeking missiles." Casts need not be long or terrifically accurate; the shark will generally find any fly within a five-foot radius. Once the shark chomps down on the fly, get ready: Some fish will take out three or four hundred yards of line in a run and are celebrated for their astounding leaps, which can reach twenty feet above the water!

There is a sense of bravado in big-game fishing, and the audacity to chase mako sharks with a fly rod only ups the ante. Yet Conway's eagerness to have his clients stick a shark is balanced by a great admiration and respect for these animals—and a desire to cease their senseless slaughter by "sportsmen." To this end, he's launched Flying Mako, a catch and release fly-fishing tournament where proceeds go toward shark conservation efforts. He has also tried to persuade by example.

"I got to know a commercial fisherman who caught and killed a lot of sharks with a handline," Conway recalled. "I think he thought I was one step above the village idiot, casting to them with a fly rod. One time we were fishing pretty close by each other, and I hooked a shark. It nearly jumped into his boat. He came over afterwards and said, 'Boy I thought I fished light tackle!' We moored our boats at the same marina, and he'd come over some days and ask how I did. When he decided that I wasn't a threat to what he was doing, he began to share hints about where to find the sharks on certain tides. This began to bring the mako's behavior into context for me.

"I changed marinas and didn't see him for a number of years, and then I ran into him. He told me that he'd gotten out of commercial fishing—killing makos just started to feel weird. 'I want to do what you do—take people out to catch makos so they can see what great adversaries they are, then put them back.' After his first trip, he stopped by my house to tell me about his day. 'I had two kids and a dad, and we released ten makos. I apologized to every fish before I let it go for all the sharks I killed. Seeing the look on those kids' faces when we got the sharks up to the boat— I've never had a better day on the water in my life.'"

Conway has ambivalent feelings about fly fishing on television. "It's a weird dynamic," he reflected. "A big part of the reason that I like to fish is a chance to get away from crowds and be alone with my thoughts. When we're filming a segment, it's not my space anymore, as I have all the crew along, and I need to remember that I'm not just fishing; we're making a program. But on the other hand, I love the idea that the program may be inspiring viewers to go out and do something that's brought me so much satisfaction—to go out and fly fish for carp, or a shark, or a steelhead, or a bluegill. Each fish is unique and presents challenges in its own way, whether it's a six-inch brook trout or a six-foot mako shark. I don't discount any species, as long as it's caught on a fly rod and done in a sporting manner. For me, it's all thrilling and all connected. It's about the journey."

ABOUT THE ANGLER

CONWAY BOWMAN is the owner and operator of Bowman Bluewater. He began fly fishing in Idaho at eight years old. Since then he's mastered the river, lake, and sea. He has hosted ESPN's *In Search of Flywater* and is now the host of *Fly Fishing the World* on the Sportsman Channel. Conway is the current International Game Fish Association (IGFA) world-record holder of redfish on ten-pound test—a 41.65-pound bull. He lives in the San Diego area with his wife, Michelle, and son, Maximillian.

LISA CUTTER
Getting away from the chatter in your mind

LISA CUTTER AND HER HUSBAND RALPH have made a career as fly-fishing instructors. It seems fitting that her entrée to the sport started with a lesson.

"When I met Ralph, neither of us had really fly fished," Lisa began. "We did a little fishing together with spinning rods and a fly with a bubble, but we were more interested in rock climbing and hiking. We were living in Squaw Valley, California, at the time, and we saw a flyer for a fly-fishing class. We took it on a pure whim. It turned out that the class was being taught by the late Mel Krieger, one of the great fly-fishing teachers of his generation. We had no idea who Mel was at the time, but we decided that we enjoyed fly fishing, and it was quickly an important part of our lives."

At the same time that fly fishing touched Lisa's and Ralph's lives, they began their long love affair with the Sierra—the mountains that naturalist John Muir called "the range of light." "For our honeymoon, we hiked the California stretch of the Pacific Crest Trail," Lisa continued. "When you're living in the Sierra for five months—getting up with the sun, going to bed with the sun—you really get in touch with the Sierra cycle. That experience helped set the stage for the lives we have today. We've fished many places around the world, and they've all been beautiful and intriguing in their own way. But if I had to pick one place that's beautiful and has great fishing, it would be right here in the Sierra Nevada."

LEFT
The lakes of the High Sierra hold a special appeal for Lisa Cutter.

Lisa and Ralph had no grand vision of starting a fly-fishing school as they became more enamored of the sport. "I guided for a while but found it unfulfilling," Lisa said. "I wasn't that interested in putting people into numbers of fish. I wanted to teach people *how* to fish. You have an opportunity to do this when you're guiding, but people may have different expectations. There was one outing that really turned me off on guiding. I had a guy out on the Truckee River, and he landed five really nice fish. That's a pretty good day on the Truckee, but the angler was really bummed out. I just didn't get it. It was a spectacularly beautiful day and the guy was getting fish, but it wasn't enough.

"At the time we started the school (California School of Flyfishing), there weren't really any fly-fishing schools around. Without a blueprint to work from, it just sort of evolved. The school format was attractive not only for the teaching focus; it would allow us to create a more predictable schedule so we could get our own fishing in! We offer both introductory and advanced classes; I do all the intro classes. I really enjoy the chance to turn people on to fishing. Some of the seasoned anglers in the advanced classes can be a little jaded, but not the beginners. Some know next to nothing—I've had students who didn't realize there were aquatic insects in the river—but they have the desire to learn. Some of the students are billionaires; some have saved for two years to be able to attend. People from all walks of life can come together over fly fishing. I get as excited as the students do; it's a great privilege to be able to introduce someone to something that you cherish. There's nothing more rewarding than reaching the end of a class and seeing your students bursting with excitement. I'll sometimes get letters or emails from people I taught years back thanking me for opening up a new spiritual part of their life."

In many parts of the world, California's best-known fish is the rainbow trout; it was McCloud River rainbows and Russian River steelhead, after all, that were shipped south to Patagonia and west to New Zealand to populate those region's rivers. Yet it's the diminutive and strikingly colored California golden trout (*Oncorhynchus aguabonita aguabonita*) that's recognized as the state fish. Goldens—believed to have evolved from redband rainbows that colonized the Kern River drainage in the southern Sierras—are present in some three hundred lakes and more than two hundred miles of streams in the Golden State. (The fish have been introduced into many of these systems.) The pursuit of golden trout in the high country is a perfect fusion of Lisa's loves of backpacking and fishing. "Once or twice a year, Ralph and me will head into the High Sierras to pursue these little gems," she added. "They are so beautiful, and the places where you find them are that much more remote. You have to work a little bit more to get there, but that makes the reward that much richer. In the end, it's all about the adventure."

There are many ways you can derive enjoyment from a fishing trip: catching a big fish, catching a lot of fish, catching a fish you really had to work for, or as Lisa described, not fishing at all. "When we lived in Truckee full-time, we'd take our dinner and a bottle of wine down to the river four or five times a week in the summer. We had plenty of good dinner spots if someone happened to be in the water when we arrived at one. When you know the river as well as we do, having dinner there is as good as fishing. You can just take it all in and lose yourself as you gaze at the expanse of the river, or focus on the minutiae, the bugs, the close-up patterns on the rocks. Either way it sucks you in, offering up some of my life's purest moments. You realize at these times that fishing is, at least in part, merely an excuse to take us out to the river.

"I've meditated for thirty-seven years. It's a way I can lose myself for a time, a method for getting away from the chatter that's in my mind. I think for many people who take up fly fishing, the attractiveness of the sport is the same as what I find in meditation—for the time you're on the river, it gets you away from the chatter in your mind."

ABOUT THE ANGLER

LISA CUTTER operates California School of Flyfishing (www.flyline.com) with her husband, Ralph, from Nevada City and Truckee, California. She and Ralph have produced the DVD *Bugs of the Underworld* and have been profiled in *National Geographic Adventure*, the *Los Angeles Times*, *Outside*, the *New York Times*, the *Wall Street Journal*, *Sunset*, and *Playboy*. Though they've fly fished the world, they remain devoted to their home waters in the Sierra Nevada.

KIRK DEETER
Tinkering with fish

KIRK DEETER BEGAN FLY FISHING FOR LOVE. Initially it was for the love of a woman, not a fish.

"I met Sarah, who would eventually be my wife, at the University of Michigan," Kirk began. "Her family was from Michigan, and her father/grandfather/great-grandfather had all fly fished. It was quite a family tradition. They had a cabin on the Pere Marquette River in the western part of the state, and I first took up the sport to curry favor with my in-laws. The first time I got in the river with a fly rod, I disappeared for many hours—I was so smitten with it. My in-laws thought I'd gotten lost; they sent my wife out to find me!

"If you're a thoughtful person, fly fishing has a natural appeal. The wheels have to be turning upstairs for things to work. I like fixing things, tinkering with things. Some people do it with cars and engines. I like to do it with fish. Fly fishing is a great puzzle; it's about problem solving. Every day you wake up and the puzzle pieces are splayed out differently. No matter what tips and tricks you've figured out, there's always something new waiting around the next bend."

LEFT
An angler launches a cast at Beaver Island, Lake Michigan— one of Kirk Deeter's favorite carping spots.

As an editor-at-large for Field & Stream, Kirk has the chance to cover a variety of fly-fishing experiences. He sees a tremendous dichotomy between fly fishing in salt water and in sweet. "Both activities utilize a fly rod, but to me, the similarities stop there," Kirk continued. "They're two different sports. On the flats, it's the cast that's most important; on a trout stream, your cast is often only twenty or thirty feet, but the presentation has more nuance. I love high-country trout fishing—there's a reason I live in the Colorado Rockies. But my world thundered and turned when I hooked my first tarpon on a fly. I like to say that I daydream of trout, but at night I dream of tarpon! There's something to be appreciated about both species—all species, for that matter. It's amazing to catch a tarpon, to come in contact with a creature that might be as old as you or older (tarpon can live to eighty years), a fish that's been dodging bull sharks and red tides to survive. Likewise, it's very satisfying to fool a trout. They're such beautiful creatures, with their elaborate scales. When you're trout fishing, you're not matching wits against one fish; you're up against tens of thousands of years of instinct that's constantly evolving."

Over the years Kirk has become a champion of fly fishing for what has historically been considered a somewhat less romantic species—carp. In some ways his feelings about carp encapsulate what he loves about fly fishing in general, and where he sees the future of the sport. "I've had the chance to go all over the world and catch many different species, but it's turned out that one of the most interesting fly-rod targets is swimming right in my backyard," Kirk said. "I guess it's a case where familiarity has bred contempt…or used to! I think carp are maligned here because they're not considered classic table fare—though they were brought to North America in the 1800s specifically for that purpose. Carp have many qualities to commend them. They are one of the most resilient fish in the world. They can live in almost any conditions—warm or cold, clean or dirty water—and are readily accessible just about wherever you live. Go to a local lake or a golf course pond, and carp are the fish you're likely to see. Not everyone has the time or money to travel to the Bahamas or Key West to find tailing bonefish or cruising tarpon. If you want to sight cast to a tailing fish that might be ten pounds or more, carp are it. Carp are able to communicate with each other; if you spook one, you'll probably need to find another spot, as the spooked fish will send out a warning to others nearby, and they'll be off the bite.

"For me, carp create a complex problem-solving matrix in your head. With tarpon, the matrix is simple: You see the tarpon, you make the cast. If you put the fly three feet in front of the fish and make a good strip, the fly will probably get eaten. With carp, you're thinking about many things: How are they swimming? Are they 'cruisers,' swimming along the bottom? Are they 'feeders,' tipped nose down (obviously rooting for food)? Or are they suspended higher in the water column? Each type of carp demands its own type of cast, fly, and presentation.

"Carp really get your wheels spinning. I like to equate carp fishing with soccer. Around the world, carp is the number-one sport fish. A staggering amount of money is spent on carp angling. There are carp in ponds in England and France that are mourned when they die; hundreds of people might pay tens of thousands of dollars for a chance to come fish for it. But here in America, it's just starting to catch on."

Many of fly fishing's skills can be taught—casting, entomology, fly tying, to name a few. But there's one quality—some might call it "fishyness" and others might call it instinct—that's harder to impart. It's safe to say that Kirk Deeter has it. He has reason to believe that his son Paul may have it, too. "There's a little creek right across from our house that has small brook trout," Kirk explained. "From time to time in the summer I'll take my son Paul over there with a tenkara rod. [Tenkara is the traditional Japanese method of fly fishing using just a long rod and fly line, which is attached directly to the tip of the rod; it's ideal for making delicate presentations on small mountain streams.] I put that long rod in his hands, and stood back as he went creeping along the creek bank like a lion cub, very wary so as not to spook fish. You can't learn that sort of instinct; like a bird dog, you either have it or you don't. Watching him crawl along the bank was one of my proudest and happiest moments. It looked like I was going to have a future fishing partner."

ABOUT THE ANGLER

KIRK DEETER is an editor-at-large for *Field & Stream* magazine and editor of *Trout*, the publication of Trout Unlimited. He is also the editor-in-chief of *Angling Trade* and senior editor of *The Flyfish Journal*. His stories have appeared in *Garden & Gun, The Drake, 5280, Fly Rod & Reel, Fly Fisherman, Big Sky Journal, SaltWater Sportsman,* and *Trout,* among other places. Kirk is also the coauthor of three books: *The Little Red Book of Fly Fishing* (with Charlie Meyers); *Castworks: Reflections of Fly Fishing Guides and the American West* (Game & Fish Mastery Library) (with Andrew W. Steketee and Liz Steketee); and *Tideline: Captains, Fly-Fishing and the American Coast* (with Andrew W. Steketee and Marco Lorenzetti).

SENATOR MIKE ENZI
It means more than talk

THERE'S A COMMON REFRAIN AMONG ANGLERS about the old time/money conundrum: When you're young you have a lot of time to fish, but not necessarily enough financial resources to get to where you want to fish. Later in life when the bank balances are a bit more in the black, you no longer have the time. It's not much different for a U.S. senator.

"Since coming to Washington, I get lots of offers to fish with people," Senator Mike Enzi began, "but I don't get many chances to take them up on their offers. Even though I get back to Wyoming most weekends, I don't have much downtime. I generally have three to five meetings a day with constituents in three to five towns. In Wyoming, towns are pretty spread out. That means a lot of time driving around. I certainly had a lot more time to fish before I got this job, but I've figured out one way to sneak in a little fishing. I have a travel rod that I always carry with me. If we're driving along a road that happens to border a trout stream, I'll try to pull over and fish for an hour here and there. I've learned that spots right along the road can be pretty good places to fish. Other anglers often ignore those spots, thinking they've been overfished, and that they'd be better served pushing further away. My roadside fishing has reinforced my commitment to using barbless hooks. It's certainly better for safely releasing fish, but it's also good for releasing constituents. During my

LEFT
The upper Snake River, with the Tetons in the background—one of Senator Enzi's favorite Wyoming streams.

roadside stops, passersby will pull over and approach the river to give me their opinion on one issue or another. I'm always concerned that I'll catch people on my back cast. By using barbless hooks, I figure I should be able to get the fly free from their hat or clothing before the press arrives."

The importance of barbless hooks is one lesson Senator Enzi has taken away from the river. He touched upon a few others. "I've learned a lot of patience on the water, and the need for inventiveness," he continued. "You need to be flexible in your approach, as what works one day may not work the next. That ability to be flexible certainly comes in handy in the legislative process. Fly fishing has also shown me how we sometimes try to make things more complicated than they need to be. I remember taking my son Brad up to the Bighorn Mountains when he was about five to show him how to fish. We were on a small stream, and he was flailing away. I said, "Brad, if you keep thrashing the water like that, you're not going to catch anything." Those words had hardly left my mouth before he yelled, "Dad, I got one!" It doesn't always have to be scientific and technical. This perception of fly fishing drives some people away from the sport. Sometimes it's just about learning the joys of being on the river. Fly fishing is my getaway time. I love the sound of the stream, the birds, the wind rustling through the trees. In Wyoming, there's always wind. You have to learn how to work with it if you're going to fish here."

Senator Enzi's beloved Wyoming rivers—the Snake, the North Platte, the Wind— are a long way from the Russell Office Building on C Street and Constitution Avenue. Yet there are enough fishing trappings in Senator Enzi's chambers to keep the lure of the river alive. "I have my grandfather's fly rod, my first fly reel (an automatic), my dad's creel and a Jeff Abel Measure Net, which makes it easy to see how big of a fish you caught," the Senator described. "The disadvantage of the net is that once you release the fish to grow more, it can't grow in your mind, as you've measured it! I have a few fish on the wall—a hand-carved wooden rainbow trout and a salmon fashioned from granite and soapstone—and three fly-fishing paintings. I also have a shadow box with some flies tied by a friend, Ron Hayes, whom I work with on OSHA issues. Ron had a son who died in a grain elevator accident. The flies he sent me were tied with the feathers from the last duck that his son shot." (Senator Enzi is ranking member on the Senate Health, Education, Labor, and Pensions Committee.)

Occasionally, fishing opportunities do present themselves a bit closer to the Hill. "In April there's an event called the Jim Range National Casting Call," the senator explained. "It's held on the Potomac at the time when the shad are running. Members of the House and Senate have a chance to go fishing and learn about fisheries management issues. One year, Lefty Kreh was giving casting lessons on the grass by the river. I saw him cast fifty feet with just the top fourteen inches of a rod. Another year, the event timing hit the shad run perfectly. Everyone who was out there was getting six or eight fish an hour—that's about all you can land in an hour, as they fight hard. Some House members missed a vote. Since that time, organizers have tried to schedule the Casting Call *near* the peak of the run."

Though Senator Enzi politely declines most of the fishing offers he receives, one occasionally comes along that's simply too good to refuse. "I had always wanted to be on ESPN when I was younger," he recalled, "but I guess I wasn't athletic enough. A few years back, the network contacted me to see if I would be willing to film a fly-fishing piece with them. I said that if they'd shoot it in Wyoming, I'd do it. We got to a spring creek I know with the camera crew, and the trout were feeding like crazy on the surface. The director asked me to pose by the pickup truck and explain the day's fishing. I said, 'No, you don't understand. The fish are jumping *now*!' But we ended up doing it his way. When I got down to the water, the fish were still feeding. On my first cast, I hooked a twenty-one-inch cutthroat—good size for a cutthroat. The morning continued that way. We were scheduled to shoot for two days, but by noon on day one we had everything we needed and they were ready to quit. I wanted to keep fishing.

"Sometimes when I'm back in Wyoming and stop into a restaurant for breakfast or lunch, a constituent will come up and say 'I saw you on TV this morning.' I'll ask 'What was I talking about?' They'll say 'You weren't talking, you were fishing.'

"That counts for a lot more in Wyoming than talk."

ABOUT THE ANGLER

MICHAEL B. ENZI was sworn in as Wyoming's twentieth United States Senator on January 7, 1997. He's made a name on Capitol Hill for his unique way of breaking down party lines and working across the aisle. Senator Enzi believes that people can agree on 80 percent of the issues 80 percent of the time and if they leave the other 20 percent out they can get a lot done. With that mentality he has turned one of the most contentious Senate committees (Health, Education, Labor, and Pensions) into one of the most productive. Before joining the U.S. Senate, Senator Enzi served two terms as mayor of Gillette, Wyoming, three terms as state representative, and a term as state senator. He is an elder in the Presbyterian Church and taught high school Sunday school class for more than ten years. Senator Enzi's love for Wyoming grew as he became an Eagle Scout. He has been honored as a Distinguished Eagle by Scouts and Significant Sig by Sigma Chi Fraternity. He is an avid hunter, fly fisher, bicyclist, and reader. Senator Enzi is married and has three children and five grandchildren. His favorite trout stream is Wyoming's Wind River.

BILL FORD
Figuring it out on your own

FICTIONAL CHARACTERS from Hemingway's Nick Adams ("Big Two-Hearted River") to Tom McGuane's James Quinn (The Sporting Club) have found a certain solace and catharsis on the rivers of northern Michigan. It was little different for Bill Ford.

"My parents belonged to a fishing club up north, though neither of them particularly loved to fish," Bill began. "For them, it was more of a legacy thing. My mother would take me up there when I was a young boy, and the caretaker and manager for the club—a wonderful gentleman—took an interest in me. He would take me on walks through the woods and I would ask him millions of questions; it probably drove him crazy, but he never let on as much. On one of those walks, he took me to the river and introduced me to fly fishing. He'd make the cast and hook the fish and let me reel it in. I fell in love with fishing immediately. I was about four years old at the time. When I was asked what I wanted for my birthday, I would say that I wanted to go up to the club and go fishing. When I got my driver's license, I would head up nearly every weekend to fish.

"I remember the caretaker telling me once that there were four phases of fishing:

Phase One—When you want to catch a fish
Phase Two—When you want to catch a lot of fish

Phase Three—When you want to catch a big fish

Phase Four—When you just want to be able to fish

"That bit of wisdom has always stuck with me."

Bill has been fortunate to fish all over the world. Though the rivers off Katmai National Park & Preserve and their five species of salmon, char, grayling, and out-sized rainbow trout have their pull, Bill is just as happy to fish diminutive streams closer to home. "My favorite fishing is on smaller water, with a three- or four-weight rod," he continued. "I almost exclusively fish dry flies, even if conditions aren't quite right. And I prefer to fish on my own, without a guide, whenever possible. Experimenting with different flies and techniques and figuring things out on my own is a big part of the satisfaction I get from fly fishing. I like to do it my way, even if it means catching fewer fish."

Ford Motor Company was an early adopter of green business initiatives, from establishing a wildlife habitat at one of its plant locations to incorporating 25 percent postconsumer materials in its plastic parts to launching the world's first hybrid-electric sport utility vehicle. Much of this pro-environment vision can be attributed to Bill. "Within the auto industry, I am known as one of the earliest green advocates," he said, "and I took criticism for it early on. When I think back to the source of my passion for the environment, there is no doubt it is from my early days out in the wild, standing in rivers. My fly-fishing experiences formed my viewpoint of the natural world and helped me understand why it is worth preserving." Though fly fishing has helped inform Ford's business practices, business does not make its way to the river. "I make it a point to not mix business and fly fishing," Bill explained. "For me, fishing is a private thing, a personal thing. It is something I do by myself, with close friends or with my sons. I do not want to be worrying about business when I am out on the river."

It should come as no surprise that someone whose family business has involved the creation of something as complex, precise, and stylish as an automobile might have more than a passing interest in craftsmanship and engineering. Befitting a fly angler, Bill has a design interest in fly rods…so much so that he ended up buying a fly-rod manufacturer. "I had long been a fan of Scott Fly Rods, which was founded by a man named Harry Wilson. I was on a business trip in England, and happened to read that Harry had had a stroke, and the future of the company was unknown. I wrote his wife a letter saying I would be interested in keeping the company going. I returned to the states, and a few days later, flew out to the Bay Area (where Scott was formerly based) and met with Harry and his wife. He decided to sell Scott to me.

"I am the first to admit that I am not a rod designer, but I really love giving Jimmy Bartschi (Scott's designer) my feedback on new prototypes. The trend in the industry has been toward stiffer and faster sticks, but I have always been a fan of softer, slower-action rods. They are much better suited for small-stream trout fishing. It has been fun to have a chance to fish the prototypes as well as some of the early Scott designs."

Bill may eschew a guide's assistance on his river trips, but playing guide is another matter—especially when the clients are his boys. "Teaching both of my sons to fly fish has provided me with tremendous satisfaction. I become the guide, wading next to them in the river. Watching them discover the sport is more fun than fishing myself."

ABOUT THE ANGLER

WILLIAM CLAY (BILL) FORD JR. is executive chairperson of Ford Motor Company. He joined Ford's board of directors in 1988 and has been its chairperson since January 1999. He serves as chair of the board's finance committee and as a member of the sustainability committee. He also served as chief executive officer of the company from October 2001 to September 2006, when he was named executive chairperson. Bill's charitable, volunteer, and business efforts are highlighted by his commitment to the city of Detroit. As vice chairperson of the Detroit Lions professional football team, he led efforts to build a new, environmentally friendly stadium in Detroit that was the site of Super Bowl XL. Through Detroit Lions Charities, Bill helped develop the Detroit Police Athletic League youth football program into one of the largest in the country. He is chairperson of the board of the Detroit Economic Club, a member of the board of trustees of both the Henry Ford Health System and The Henry Ford, a member of the board of directors of eBay Inc., and chair of the New Michigan Initiative of Business Leaders for Michigan. Bill also is a founding partner of Fontinalis Partners, LLC, a Michigan-based investment firm that acts as a strategic operating partner to transportation infrastructure technology companies around the world. An avid fly fisher and car enthusiast, Bill enjoys playing hockey and tennis, and he is a black belt in the martial art of tae kwon do.

JOHN GIERACH
Learning something new

"I CAME OUT WEST IN 1968," John Gierach began. "I don't know why I came out, I just did; after all, it was the sixties, and we were hippies. I think I'd seen two people fly fishing before I moved to Colorado. There was a cadre of people in the Midwest who fly fished for bass. I'd always fished as a boy with my father and uncle in Minnesota but hadn't done any fly fishing. I heard the spectrum of opinions on the pastime. From my father: 'That's the real art.' From my Uncle Leonard: 'Those guys are conceited pricks who never catch anything.' Out in Colorado, people were doing it. I thought I'd take it up. It was a pretty thing to watch, and I thought it would be fun. I went to a yard sale and bought a four- or five-piece Wright & McGill fiberglass spin/fly combo rod with a reversible reel seat, a Pflueger reel, and a level wind reel. I still have the reel.

"In those days you didn't have instructional videos or fly-casting classes. Being a hippie, I had lots of time, and tried to learn by myself. Fishermen were generally friendlier than now. As I was slogging away, old guys would come up—'Excuse me, can I make a suggestion?' With their help, I kind of pieced it together. Most of us aren't geniuses; we plod along doing the best we can. If you're observant, you pick up on what's going on, slowly but surely. I remember a time when I struggled with fly fishing. But then there came a time when I could walk up to a river and know what to do—know where the fish would be, what fly to tie on, etc."

LEFT
John Gierach has enjoyed learning to catch steelhead in recent years. Here, an angler prepares to spey cast on Oregon's Deschutes River.

John Gierach may be the world's best-known, most beloved fly-fishing writer, though the path to writing about fishing was not nearly as clear and direct as his prose. "People ask me, 'Were you a fisherman or a writer first?' Sometimes I answer 'Yes.' The truth is, it was an embarrassingly long time before I put the two together. I always wanted to be a writer and worked hard at writing before becoming a serious fisherman. I starting writing in high school and have been a lifelong reader. When I moved to Colorado, I was trying to do poetry and fiction. I was publishing a poem here and there in literary magazines, but there was no money in it. I was driving a garbage truck at the time to make ends meet. I used to read *Fly Fisherman* magazine—it was the only fly-fishing publication around at that time—and at one point, it occurred to me that they were paying writers for this stuff, and it didn't look that hard. I submitted a piece, and it was accepted. I made a month's wages—maybe seventy-five dollars—for the story. It just took off from there. I remember thinking at the time that doing fly-fishing articles was a way I could make money while pursuing my 'actual' literary career. Then I started stumbling upon the writing of Tom McGuane, Russell Chatham, and Charles Waterman. I learned from these guys, especially McGuane, that you can write about fly fishing in a substantial manner as much as you can write about anything else in a substantial manner. They don't have to be separate. There's another valuable lesson I learned, this time from the writing of John McPhee: You get at your subject by the people who do it, and you get to people by the subject they're interested in.

"Sometimes people will say 'I wish I were you, you get to fish for a living!' Sometimes I'll respond, 'You're right, it's my job.' But I'm only half kidding. I need to fish to get material. I can't sit around and make this stuff up."

Coming of fly-fishing age in Colorado, John has gravitated toward trout fishing. But he's very open toward targeting other species. "I never thought of fly fishing as exclusively a trout thing," he said, "though they go together well. I think people fall in love with the method more than the fish. I was an early follower of Dave Whitlock when he was going around talking about bass fishing with a fly rod. I was doing it when a lot of fly fishers looked down at any species that wasn't trout. I think it was Jim Harrison who said bass were merely 'a hyperactive carp'; there was a mindset that anything that wasn't a salmonid was a trash fish. I should add that I like fishing for carp, though it was more fun when people looked down on them! Thanks to my bass fishing, some of my trout-fishing friends called me 'Grits' after Grits Gresham (a host of *American Sportsman* and author of *The Complete Book of Bass Fishing*).

"I've taken up steelhead fishing in the last few years, in part so I could take up spey casting. I thought it would be cool to throw a lot of line. A friend that tagged along said, 'It's fun to be doing something new, but it's annoying to be a beginner again after all this time.' That didn't bother me. I got to experience all the fun of learning something new, figuring out the kind of water the fish might lie in and what flies to use…or that it didn't really matter that much what fly I tied on! A few years ago I fished on the Klickitat River in Washington with Jeff Cottrell, a very knowledgeable guide on the river. He didn't stand at my shoulder. He just put me on the water. If I didn't look like I knew what I was doing, he would tell me. But he didn't have to. It's not a big cosmic shot that comes when you realize you know what you're doing. One day, it's just there. This moment of realization isn't going to happen again in a big way for me with trout fishing, but it was satisfying to have it happen with steelheading.

"I believe that fishing is like life in that it's not just a series of discrete episodes, but part of a longer, larger process. On a steelhead trip last March in Oregon, we had the worst rains in recent memory, and the fishing was terrible. I was out with a fellow named Rob Russell (of Angler's Book Supply), and I learned an incredible amount from him. It was much more valuable than when I've walked right up to the river and caught fish. I got stuff that I'll be able to use down the line. That I didn't find any fish was meaningless in the big picture."

ABOUT THE ANGLER

JOHN GIERACH is the author of many books, including *No Shortage of Good Days*; *Another Lousy Day in Paradise*; *Dances with Trout*; *Fool's Paradise*; *Still Life with Brook Trout*; *At the Grave of the Unknown Fisherman*; *Death, Taxes, and Leaky Waders*; *Standing in a River Waving a Stick*; *Even Brook Trout Get the Blues*; *Where the Trout Are All as Long as Your Leg*; *Sex, Death, and Fly-Fishing*; *View From Rat Lake*; and *Trout Bum*. His work has appeared in *Gray's Sporting Journal*, *Field & Stream*, and *Fly Rod & Reel*, where he is a columnist. John also writes a column for the monthly *Redstone Review*. He lives in Lyons, Colorado.

CARL HIAASEN

Making sense of the madness

"TO ME, THE WHOLE INTOXICATION OF FLY FISHING is sight fishing," Carl Hiaasen declared. "It satisfies our primal instinct to hunt and provides the challenge of putting a fly into that tiny radius where the fish will eat it. I got hooked on sight fishing to bonefish with a fly rod when I was a teenager, when not many people were trying to do it. It's one of the more extraordinary experiences in fly fishing; success requires so much to go right. You can get the same thrill from casting to a rising trout. It's a gas trying to get a tiny fly to drift where the trout will eat it. It's not quite the same as having to hit a moving bonefish or tarpon or permit, but it requires the same concentration. There's the same connection to the water…though if you tied a trout to a bonefish, the trout would be pulled inside out!"

Carl began chasing bonefish in Biscayne Bay in high school, after an apprenticeship on the canals around his hometown of Plantation, Florida. "I had a dear friend in junior high named Bob Branham," Carl continued, "and he had a twelve-foot aluminum boat with a six-horsepower outboard. (Bob went on to become an acclaimed bonefish guide.) We'd go out in the canals and fish for bream, bass, occasionally baby tarpon. We'd read in Field & Stream about using fly rods with poppers and rubber bugs on the surface, and that's what we did. We caught a lot of fish, mostly little guys, casting into the shoreline. It taught us precision; if you're four feet too far away from the shore, the fish wouldn't come out and get it. When we could drive,

LEFT
Having the right person in the boat—be it guide or fellow angler—is an important part of a good day's fishing for Carl Hiaasen.

we'd put the johnboat on the roof and head to Biscayne Bay. A closet dowel was our push pole. We started with a spinning rod and shrimp but then switched to fly rods. I became friends with Bill Curtis, who pioneered fly fishing for bonefish in Biscayne Bay. It's still extraordinary that within sight of the Miami skyline, you can cast to twelve-, thirteen-pound bonefish. The bay gets great tidal action, and the fish seem to have adapted to having 2.5 million people on their doorstep. You don't see many tailing fish; they're in slightly deeper water."

When he moved from Miami to the Keys in the mid-nineties, Carl began hunting bonefish solo from his skiff—no easy game. "It's pretty windy down there, and you're out in the open," he explained. "You'd better get pretty good or you'll never catch anything. I'd be up on the poling platform. I had to learn to get down very quietly and quickly once I spotted a fish, and I'd have about a two-second window to get a cast off. It was very challenging." As tough as chasing bonefish alone can be, it might be preferable to having the wrong person in the boat with you.

"Fishing is not something that you want to get all your friends involved in," Carl added. "Some people will be good, some people you'll want to kill. If I'm going to spend eight hours throwing a fly at fish, I better be with someone who I enjoy." This extends to guides. "There were some legendary guides in the Keys who were a little ragged with their people skills. They'd ride clients about making a bad cast. I had this happen to me a few times, and I'd ask them to come down from the platform and make the cast themselves. They wouldn't do it. There's no excuse for a bad attitude out there. I'm very fortunate because the guides I fish with—Tim Klein, Steve Huff, Bob Branham, Beau Strathman, and a few others—are all dear friends of mine. They're not only geniuses at finding the fish, they're great company on the water. At this point in my life I don't need to spend eight hours on a boat with somebody I don't like. The experience of being out there is just too rare, and too important. A guy like Steve Huff—he fishes dawn to dusk, and if you're in his boat, he expects you to do the same. He has no problem telling you when you've screwed up a cast. But when he says nice cast, you know you've done something. Sometimes I see boats out there, and the guide is poling around in twenty-knot winds while the client is sitting drinking beer. I want to beat that sport with the push pole! The thrill is in the hunt, and you have to learn that."

In addition to the thrill of the hunt, Carl finds satisfaction in the focus that fly fishing demands. "You have to get in a rhythm, throw a nice tight loop, strike when the fish hit. You can't be thinking about anything else, or you're not likely to catch anything. It clears your brain. To do it right is just plain hard, but there's a wonderful karma to it. This total focus makes fly fishing alluring for so many people I know, especially hard-charging type-As. It's therapeutic. And it's the same if you're in a brook trout stream or a steelhead river or fishing for tarpon in Key West. Sometimes you'll come upon a guy in a drift boat flailing away like he's beating a rug. Sure, he might catch a hapless trout. But my bet is that he doesn't know why he's there. He's frenetic. He's not fishing for the right reasons. He's there because he thought it would be cool, or someone said he should try it. He's not going to stay with it; you know it. It's no different than golf. Some people play because they think they should, not because they really appreciate the game."

Having a significant other who appreciates the game of fly fishing—and its inherent ups and downs—is important for the angler's longevity…and perhaps for the relationship's longevity! "You need someone who understands that you may go out all day and come back with nothing, and doesn't bust your balls about it," Carl advised. "Because sometimes, that's what happens. Otherwise, you'll be miserable. I was down in Everglades City, Florida, tarpon fishing with Steve Huff a few years ago, and I came home with my chest covered with bruises from fighting fish. It looked like someone had beaten me with a baseball bat. You've got to have someone in your life that gets it when they see you and you look like you've been mugged, yet you're grinning ear to ear."

One of the recurring themes of Carl Hiaasen's writing is man's frayed connection with the natural world, and how important it is to remember that we're sharing the planet with other creatures. He mused on how fly fishing informs this leitmotif. "I get the chance to fish some places in Florida that probably look much like they did one thousand years ago. I have to take my impressions away from those places to get pumped up to write about the recklessness with which many politicians go about dealing with what's left of our resources. It's hard for someone who doesn't have that connection to the natural world—that dazzling world where you're being totally immersed, emotionally and physically, in the life around you—to appreciate how precious it is. I don't think I could write like I do without the connection I have to the outdoors that fly fishing has given me…especially given the kind of insanity I encounter as a columnist and novelist who's trying to make sense of the madness."

ABOUT THE ANGLER

CARL HIAASEN was born and raised in Florida. He is the author of eleven novels, including the best-selling *Nature Girl*, *Skinny Dip*, *Sick Puppy*, and *Lucky You*, and three best-selling children's books: *Hoot*, *Flush*, and *Scat*. Carl's most recent work of nonfiction is *The Downhill Lie: A Hacker's Return to a Ruinous Sport*. He also writes a weekly column for the *Miami Herald*. He was named *Fly Rod & Reel*'s Angler of the Year in 2012.

LEFTY KREH
Imparting wisdom

THE LEGIONS OF FLY ANGLERS who have looked to Lefty Kreh for half a century for guidance on everything from casting to saltwater techniques to knot tying might be surprised to learn that one of the foundations of his knowledge is his willingness to be wrong. "If I had had a more advanced education, I might have approached many challenges in life—and fishing—in a different way," Lefty said. "These limitations have compelled me to think in simple terms, and often, to learn from my mistakes. I don't accept problems as such, but as opportunities for improvement."

Lefty shared a case in point. "In the 1950s, I began studying knots. I was trying to determine if knots under contortion lose strength. At one point, I tied ninety-eight blood knots, and broke thirty right away. Six weeks later, I tied more knots and broke thirty more. The following year, I tied—and broke—more knots. Eventually, Mark Sosin and I did a book on the topic, *Practical Fishing Knots*; it went on to sell more than three hundred thousand copies. After the book came out, I was giving a presentation at a fly-fishing club in Long Beach, California. I was showing different ways that you could attach a leader to fly line. I thought I did a pretty good job, and I asked if anyone had any questions. A kid in the front row who must have been twelve put his hand up and said 'I've got a better way.' He came up and attached the leader to the fly line in about ten seconds with a nail knot. I said, 'You forget what I did. Listen to what this kid has to say.' It goes to show that you can be a 'world-class expert' and a twelve year old can teach you something. Throughout my life, I've always listened to other people's ideas and methods. I may start out doing things one way and after a while, I'll modify. Everything I do is subject to change. You're always learning; it's an unending process. I've been doing this since 1947; every day I'm out on the water, I learn something new."

One of the great allures of fly fishing for Lefty is the opportunity to identify and solve problems. Lefty shared nuggets of wisdom on a number of topics:

- **Trout fishing**—Ask yourself these questions: Where should I stand? What are the currents? How can I get drag-free drift? (Tip: It's getting the tip of the line and the leader to fall almost vertically. You'll get some slack in the line, that's how you get a drag-free float.) If I hook a big fish, where can I land him? What are the half-dozen dry flies the best local fishermen rely on?

- **Bonefishing**—Use a sixteen-foot leader on clear, calm days as fish will be wary; use an eight-foot leader on windy days to turn the fly over. If it's blowing really hard, put the fly rod down, get a cup of coffee, and read a book instead. You can't fight twenty mile per hour winds. And if you're fishing in Islamorada, bring your best game. The bonefish there have PhDs. They're fly inspectors; they can tell you who tied the fly you're using.

- **Fishing at night**—Put nail knots in the middle of the line to indicate casts of predetermined lengths so you can drop the fly where you want it to fall. (This technique also works well to show beginners how much line they need out to load the rod.)

- **Fixing a tailing loop**—Finish the cast with your hand forward. I was at a casting seminar in Florida once with Flip Pallot, and a guy sat down at my table. 'I've had a tailing loop for thirty years. You got rid of it in three minutes.' He was so grateful, he offered to do the surgical procedure to remove my acid reflux free of charge (the grateful angler was a doctor). When I started teaching casting, I realized that if I was going to correct poor casting technique, I'd need to understand how bad casts are made. Many of the great casting instructors don't know how to make bad casts, so it's hard for them to correct bad habits. They're theorizing about what makes a bad cast.

"I've caught more than one hundred species on the fly rod," Lefty continued. "Some fish—smallmouth bass, bonefish, peacock bass—have a special appeal for me. But my greatest satisfaction is putting someone at the front of the boat—an angler who has never caught the species in question, be it a tarpon, trout, or bonefish—and coaching them on how to catch that fish. It's like having the thrill of catching your first one again. This gives me much more pleasure than catching one myself. Likewise, I get great satisfaction in sharing what knowledge I've gained over time to help someone with their cast. Many people are taught to cast using just their wrist and arm—the old "ten and two" method. I don't think this is practical. You wouldn't throw a Frisbee or a spear or a ball that way. You use your body. With just a few small suggestions, I can help most people cast better in a matter of minutes."

Given his sixty-five years as an angler and his pioneering work on the flats with bonefish and tarpon, it may seem remarkable that Lefty Kreh has never won a fly-fishing tournament. There's a reason—he never competed in one. "If you compete with your fellow anglers, you become their competitor," Lefty advised. "If you help them, you become their friend."

Sage advice indeed!

ABOUT THE ANGLER

BERNARD "LEFTY" KREH is one of the most respected names in fly fishing—an icon and a legend in the fly-fishing arena. Regarded as a world-class master instructor, Lefty has taught fly-casting and fly-fishing techniques for more than sixty years. He has fished all over the world, venturing to some of the most secluded, unspoiled parts of the globe to fish some of the most elusive fish on the planet. Lefty has fished with international and national personalities such as Ernest Hemingway and Fidel Castro, and with most American presidents since the fifties. He is the most prolific and successful fishing writer in history, selling hundreds of thousands of copies of his works. Lefty has received numerous distinguished awards including the Lifetime Achievement Award by the American Sportfishing Association. In 1991, the U.S. Postal Service honored him with a postage stamp bearing the image of his famous Deceiver fly.

CRAIG MATHEWS

It's the places where trout live

CERTAIN WATERS ARE INDELIBLY ASSOCIATED WITH CERTAIN ANGLERS. When many think of Montana's Madison, it's Craig Mathews who comes to mind.

It was a rather happenstance route that took Craig to West Yellowstone. "I grew up in Michigan, around Grand Rapids," Craig explained. "In 1970, a friend of mine named Larry Dech said 'We gotta go to Montana.' He'd fished there once and had come back impressed. We went together, and the fishing was fantastic. About that time, I joined the Grand Haven (nearly a suburb of Grand Rapids) police department. I would save my overtime days and take a month off in the early fall to go out west with Larry. My wife, Jackie, was a police dispatcher in Grand Haven at that time, and we started fishing together in 1977. We went out to Montana for a few weeks in the fall of '77 and again in '78. Around Christmas that year, Jackie said out of nowhere, 'We're gonna move to Yellowstone.' My response was 'What are we going to do?' She replied, 'We'll work for the police department, fish, and have fun.' A few days later, Jackie contacted the West Yellowstone Police Department. They hired her over the phone. She handed the phone to me, and I was offered a job as a patrolman on the spot. It was all moving so fast. We flew out for an interview, and the police chief said, 'I'm leaving next week. You're going to be the new police chief.'

LEFT
Craig Mathews fishes an unnamed creek in Yellowstone National Park, his home waters.

"Pretty soon we were in West Yellowstone. I hadn't done my homework, and pretty soon we realized that the town had no money. My salary was ten thousand dollars a year; Jackie made less than minimum wage. But we decided to give it a year. I hired educated guys for the force who wanted to fly fish (and would work for less for that opportunity), and we built one of the most solid small-town departments in Montana. After a year I knew we were going to stay longer, but I had to figure out a way to augment our income, or it wasn't going to work. I had always dreamed of starting a fly-tying business that employed handicapped people. My sister had a handicap, and I understood the challenges she faced in finding meaningful work. This was the birth of Blue Ribbon Flies. The first year was a disaster. There were no support services for our handicapped tiers; I was the police chief and that left Jackie to run the business while trying to find retail accounts. Nick Lyons won't take credit, but he really helped by connecting us with some big retailers. The second year, business started taking off, and I left the police department to help run what had become a viable business. We ended up hiring nonhandicapped tiers to meet demand in the summer. Some talented tiers did time at the bench—Dick Talleur, Ron Brown, Jack Gartside, and John Juracek among them. We'd sneak in some fishing during the day and tie flies all night; it was like this all summer long. Over the years I've had the best people in the world working with me, all passionate fly fishers. Some of our employees have been with us since 1980. They're not just employees, but dear friends."

Beyond the strong ties that he's established with his coworkers, it's the connection to the natural world that fly fishing provides that's most gratifying for Craig. "Fly fishing puts me in a position to enjoy things that most people take for granted," he offered. "The sunrises and sunsets are always more beautiful on the river. It's the beauty and solitude of the places where trout live. That's why I live here. Fishing has given me the patience to take nature in, breathe it, taste it, feel it. I want to share this world with others, especially those who might not be able to enjoy it on their own. I've carried my sister and her wheelchair out into the middle of the river so she could fish and appreciate what means so much to me. I've also volunteered with Project Healing Waters (a program that provides basic fly-fishing, fly-casting, fly-tying and rod-building classes, along with clinics for wounded and injured military person-nel). Last spring I had a soldier from the program out with me. This poor fellow had lost sixty people in his platoon. I didn't think he was going to be able to have a good time; he was dealing with such psychological challenges. I remember him casting to and hooking an eleven-inch brown trout and landing it. I released the fish and he turned to me and said, 'This is the best day of my life. Thank God for you, thank God for trout.' If that doesn't make you love wild trout places, nothing will."

Craig's enthusiasm for sharing the rivers he loves with others is only exceeded by his relentless efforts to preserve those waters for future generations. One of his endur-ing conservation successes is known as the $3 Bridge Project, which preserved three miles of the Madison River corridor from development and provided permanent public fishing access to this blue-ribbon stretch. "It was 2001, and we were trying to find a conservation buyer for the land in question, the Candlestick Ranch. I had an old client from Hurricane, Utah, named Webster who called and said, 'My son Bart has never fly fished. He has no interest in it at all, but he has lots of money. He's going to be around Yellowstone soon. Why don't you take him fishing at $3 Bridge? Maybe he'll connect to the property and buy it and put it into conservation easement.' I said, 'Webster, I'll take him to the ends of the earth if there's a chance he could help us out.'

"I connected with the son, Barton. He had a full schedule, and he could only go out at nine o'clock. It was the worst time for any insect activity; a bright, sunny day, and only twenty degrees. We walked down below $3 Bridge and suited up. 'Chances are, Bart, we won't have very good fishing,' I said. 'But I'll show you how to cast, and how beautiful this valley is.' We went to my favorite run and sat down on a rock. 'It's good to watch the water for a while instead of just going out and starting to flail away,' I told him. We were sitting on the rock, and right at the tip of the rod, a sixteen-inch rainbow comes up and takes a midge. 'Did you see that?' Barton asked. 'Yes I did.' I tied on a #22 midge pattern, and Barton caught three rainbows, without getting up from the rock. As we came off the river, Barton said, 'I'm gonna do something for this property.' He didn't buy it outright, but he wrote us a sizable check.

"I saw Barton recently, and I asked him, 'Do you remember that day?' 'I sure do,' he replied. 'And I'm fly fishing now. I've lived in this beautiful part of Utah for a long time, and now I'm getting out to enjoy it with a fly rod. I think it's made me a better person.'"

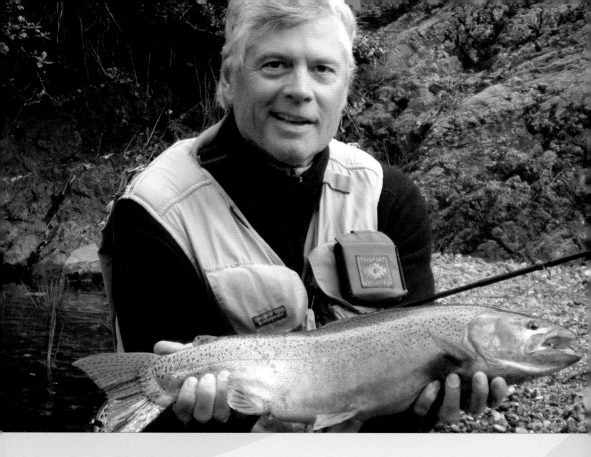

ABOUT THE ANGLER

CRAIG MATHEWS served as police chief of West Yellowstone, Montana, before opening Blue Ribbon Flies in 1980. He's gone on to become one of the great experts on western fly fishing. Craig is the author of six books, including *Fly Patterns of Yellowstone Vols 1 and 2, Fishing Yellowstone Hatches, The Yellowstone Fly-Fishing Guide, Western Fly-Fishing Strategies,* and *Fly Fishing the Madison River.* Committed to protecting and preserving wild trout habitat, Craig and Blue Ribbon Flies have received numerous awards for their conservation work from groups like the Nature Conservancy and Federation of Fly Fishers. He recently cofounded the 1% for the Planet club; member businesses donate 1 percent of gross sales to support conservation projects and have raised more than $100 million so far.

MAC MCKEEVER

Being completely out of control

UP ON THE RIGHT CORNER OF THE L.L.BEAN LETTERHEAD, there's a handsome illustration of a leaping brook trout. It's the salmon and the brook trout (*squaretail* in the local parlance) that put Maine on the angler's map more than a century ago. Thus it's with no small sense of irony that Mac McKeever—a longtime Maine resident and employee of the aforementioned outdoor retailer—swears his fishing allegiance to bass, pike, and other "brutish" fish, rather than to members of the salmonid family.

"I know that many people characterize fly fishing as a meditative pastime," Mac began. "For them, it has this Zenlike association with peace and serenity. My associations are very different. I find fly angling explosive, intense. This is likely because of the species I like to pursue—bluefish, striped bass, tarpon, pike, smallmouth and largemouth bass. There's nothing serene about a bluefish blitzing bait. For me, trout fishing just doesn't capture the thrill, the rush that you get from a smallmouth or pike hitting a popper. Some people in Maine (and other trout-fishing meccas) view bass and pike as trash fish while they sing the praises of salmonids. When I hear such naysayers, I always think of something Lefty Kreh once said—'No one ever had a heart attack catching a trout.'"

Mac still recalls the day when he was won over to fly fishing...and bass. "My dad took me fishing from an early age," he continued, "and we fished many different styles. Trolling with flies, trolling with spoons, spinning gear, in rivers, lakes, and the salt; and occasionally with a fly rod. When I was about six, we were fishing in a lake for smallmouth bass. It was a very still day, and the lake was slack calm. My dad decided to use a fly rod, and he tied on a small popping bug. I remember the visual excitement of seeing that popper get annihilated, the hole that fish punched in the water when he grabbed the fly, its jumps. I was intrigued—this gave fishing a whole different dimension than what I'd previously witnessed on the water.

"I received a fly rod the next year and continued fishing with my dad. He would mostly use spinning gear, and I would frequently use flies. As I became more proficient, flies began to prove as effective (sometimes more so) than conventional gear. After a day of bluefishing my dad began to see the light. We were on a big mud flat and could see the bluefish lazily finning around, just below the surface. Both of us were casting plugs, but we weren't having much luck. The fish didn't seem to be interested in feeding, which is rare for bluefish! I switched to a fly rod and began killing them. The flies landed a lot lighter than the plugs. The ferocity of their strikes has stayed with me. After that day both of us began spending more time with fly rods in our hands. Not only did it expand our fishing horizons, we found that it would often be a much more effective way to fish in certain situations."

Mac offered a bit more on the distinction between trout and nontrout angling. "I've been lucky enough to have some great trout-fishing experiences, to fish some of the great hatches out in Wyoming and Colorado. I think the appeal of trout fishing for many anglers is deciphering the entomology—trying to crack the case. I understand this. For me, the appeal is less about the 'figuring it out' and more about the fury of the crushing take and the exhilaration of the fight. Perhaps that's why I prefer less discriminating species of fish—fish that will take anything!"

A visceral take and scrappy battle can define a fly-fishing experience. Being able to watch it all unfold before you only heightens that adventure. One of Mac's favorite angling pursuits on his home waters in Maine is sight fishing to striped bass. "I've been a striped-bass angler since I was a boy," he continued, "but I've also long been fascinated with shallow water flats fishing, like you find in the Caribbean. The visual element, the challenge of making a very precise fly presentation, are both very compelling. I didn't think such fishing was available around Maine, and in the past would spend thousands of dollars and lots of time to travel to the Florida Keys or the Bahamas. My pursuit of stripers was typical of most other anglers—blind casting off beaches, ledges, and tidal rips in hopes of ambushing passing fish. One day I was putting my boat on the trailer after a morning of fishing, and got to chatting with a utility lineman who was having lunch by the boat launch. He mentioned a spot not far away where he'd watched big schools of large stripers patrolling an area of shallow water from his vantage point at the top of a telephone pole high on a bluff. I thanked him, backed my boat back into the water, and raced over to the spot. Sure enough, the fish were there. The clear water, combined with the white sand and dark fish, made for great visuals. It was very exciting to discover a fishery that was comparable to the exotic locales to the south so close to home. You might catch more fish casting into bait balls. But for every twenty stripers I hook blind casting, I would rather catch one sight fishing. For me, it's much more fulfilling."

When considering the "fury of the take and exhilaration of the fight," Mac logically steered the conversation to tarpon. "A fellow employee came by my office recently and told me, 'Mac, I'm going to the Keys to fish for tarpon. What's it going to be like?' I thought for a moment and said, 'I can't even describe it. It will change the way you look at fly fishing. When they eat, it's remarkable. The fish's body language tells you it's tracking the fly. As the fish rises toward the bug, its mouth opens, and you swear it could eat a soccer ball. After the eat, there are thirty seconds of pure chaos. Looking that fish in the eye as it leaps to your height (or above!), hearing the gills rattle like trash can lids banging together—it's life altering. The fishing shows and magazines don't do it justice. The surge of power will blow your mind. That first thirty seconds after a tarpon takes, you feel completely out of control—well, you *are* completely out of control.

"For most anglers, it's a wildly unfamiliar sensation to be completely out of control. You get this feeling with tarpon, mako sharks, and other giant, powerful fish. When a mako leaps clear of the water one hundred and fifty yards away, you're incredulous at how you're possibly going to be able to move this thing with a stick and some string. The power and speed of these truly wild animals is humbling. They're like beasts out of a children's book."

ABOUT THE ANGLER

MAC MCKEEVER is a senior public relations representative for L.L.Bean, Inc., a $1.5 billion multichannel specialty outdoor retailer. He represents the fishing, hunting, and outdoor gear and apparel divisions across the catalog, Internet, and retail channels. Prior to that, Mac headed up all of the advertising, marketing, and public relations activities for the L.L.Bean Outdoor Discovery Schools, a 27,000-participant-per-year outfitter. He is the president of the Coastal Conservation Association of Maine, as well as a national executive board member with Coastal Conservation Association National. He is also on the Atlantic States Fisheries Commission with the Coastal Conservation Association. Mac serves on the boards of the Maine Tourism Association and the Convention and Visitors Bureau of Greater Portland, as well as being an advisory board member with the American Fly Fishing Trade Association. Mac also has a seat on the Sport Fishing and Boating Partnership Council. He is a 25-ton master licensed captain with the United States Coast Guard. An avid outdoorsman, Mac enjoys upland bird hunting and particularly fly fishing. When he's not chasing tarpon, Mac loves to stalk striped bass on the sand flats near his home in Portland, Maine.

FRANK MOORE
The river is part of me

"A FEW YEARS AGO, I was being interviewed for a television program called *Legends of Rod & Reel*," Frank Moore began. "At one point, the director asked me, 'What were your thoughts when the ramp of the landing craft went down and you were about to land at Normandy?' My reply was, 'I thought of two things. One was my beautiful wife, Jeanne. The other was my Montague fly rod, which I had purchased just prior to leaving home.' The director came unglued when I said 'I don't know which thought came first.'"

Frank and Jeanne have a very close relationship and are coming up on their seventieth wedding anniversary as of this writing. That the Montague ranked *nearly as high* as Jeanne in Frank's thoughts says something about how much fly fishing has meant in his life.

Frank credits his father for his lifelong interest in the sport. "My dad was an ardent fly angler in the 1920s. He made his own fly lines from cuttyhunk (linen) and linseed oil and varnish, which he applied by hand. One of my first memories is of fly lines strung up all over the garage, drying. We lived in Carlton, Oregon, then. Every weekend, we'd get in the car and go out somewhere trout fishing. The limit then was at least forty-five trout. When summer came we'd take off and travel all around the state of Oregon and the Pacific Northwest to fly fish. Dad loved to find a stream that no one had been on before. Some of the places that we went, I don't know how we got there; at times we'd be driving on trails. My dear old mother was always a great sport. She loved the outdoors; I have such fond memories of her when she was in her eighties sitting on the bank with a rod in her hand (she didn't fly fish then), waiting for a fish to strike. She was a remarkable lady; wherever we went, she went right along with us. One of my fondest memories was catching a big sea run cutthroat out of Nestucca River when I was three years old. It was larger than any fish dad caught that day, and no, it was not caught on a fly."

Frank was just nine when his father died, and the family moved to the east side of the Willamette Valley. Though his dad's passing was difficult ("For a period of time, I wouldn't admit that my dad was dead," he shared), Frank kept fishing. "When I graduated from high school, I got a Montague fly rod," Frank continued. "It was my treasure, though in truth, it was an awful rod. It didn't matter too much. I was a natural caster; I had been a pretty good athlete and had good timing and coordination, and that's what casting is. The key is to let the rod do the work. Today it's a little easier to cast well, as most of the rods on the market are pretty good."

Not long after returning from Europe in 1945, Frank and Jeanne moved south to Roseburg. His love affair with the North Umpqua and its wild runs of steelhead would begin soon after. "I had seen the river once when I was a boy on a trip we took before dad died," Frank recalled. "Even as a kid, I was taken with how beautiful it was. When we moved to Roseburg, I'd be up on the river whenever I had a spare moment. The North Umpqua is an ethereal place, a little bit of heaven on earth; well, a lot of heaven! Over the years, the river has become part of me. I think of it a little like Eden after Adam and Eve's fall; even though it's not as pristine as it used to be, it's still a great place."

It wasn't long before Frank's livelihood became enmeshed with the river. "In the late forties, Clarence Gordon (who operated the North Umpqua Lodge) asked if I would like to guide for him," Frank continued. "I hadn't been on the river long, but

I was an adept angler and could cover ground. I would literally run up and down the river in my waders to learn the pools and holding water. I was never sure if Clarence thought I'd make a good guide or merely wanted me with his clients so I would not be fishing the best pools for myself, but I began guiding. The lodge closed in 1951 (thanks in large part to the building of a dam upstream, which severely impacted water flows and caused severe siltation for several years). In 1957, Jeanne and I had the chance to buy the Forest Service lease from Clarence Gordon to operate the business on the site, which was then a store/gas station. We did it. At the same time we moved to Steamboat, one of the contractors who'd been working with his crew building the road (Highway 138) along the river up to Diamond Lake left his D-8 Cat at the store. He knew I could operate it, and he said that I could feel free to use it. I leveled off a spot in back of the store, above the river, and built a few cabins. That was the start of the Steamboat Inn. Through my fishing and Steamboat Inn, I've met some of the most wonderful people in the world." Frank and Jeanne operated Steamboat until 1975. Known for its "fisherman's dinners" in the summer and its hospitable attitude to anglers, Steamboat Inn continues to be a welcome stop for visiting steelheaders.

Generations of the North Umpqua's steelhead have learned to fear the sight of Frank Moore on the bank and the hypnotic appeal of one of his untrimmed muddler minnows or Skunks skittering across the surface. When he lands a fish today he wonders how many of its ancestors he had released to spawn. Yet Frank has done more to secure the fish's well-being than anyone. "The logging in the upper reaches of the watershed started in 1954, after the road went in," Frank explained. "The little tribs up there used to have thousands of little salmonids. I took the temperature of those tribs at that time, and for years after. Thanks to the logging alongside of and over the streams, the temps climbed twenty or thirty degrees. Instead of salmonids, the tribs had dace and chubs. I started blowing the whistle with the U.S. Forest Service, Bureau of Land Management, and State Department of Forestry, and I had the documentation to back it up. Many state agencies will tell the public that they put the fish high on their agenda, but often they'll circumvent what's right for the fishery resource.

"When the state decided that they were going to put hatchery steelhead in the North Umpqua, I initially thought it would be great. After the second return, I felt it was awful. The hatchery fish don't have the same body configuration as the natives. They're a mess, and most fight like an old boot. They're a different fish. I collared a biologist one day and told him, 'I bet you a thousand dollars I can tell a hatchery fish from a wild fish on the end of my line in five seconds.' He said he didn't have that kind of money. I suggested one hundred dollars, then one dollar. Finally he said 'The average person doesn't know the difference,' and that was that. His attitude was disappointing."

In times of great stress, it's human nature to gain comfort by putting ourselves—at least mentally—in a place of calm and happiness. Frank shared one such moment of escape from nearly seventy years ago. "After we broke out of Normandy, my division (the U.S. Army's 83rd Infantry Division) was heading up the Brittany peninsula. At one point, east of the city of Dinard, we crossed a bridge that spanned a river. Down below, on the banks of the river, was a restaurant, and in front of the restaurant there was a beautiful Atlantic salmon, hanging from a hook. I can see it in my mind clear as day; it's stuck with me all these years. I remember thinking as we raced on, 'I wish I could stop and find a fly rod and try to catch one of those magnificent fish.' It took me away from where I was to a very different realm. It didn't last long, but for a few moments I was in a different place."

ABOUT THE ANGLER

FRANK MOORE is the most celebrated angler on one of the world's most celebrated steelhead rivers, the North Umpqua. Frank began guiding on the river more than sixty years ago and has led many dignitaries to the river's fabled pools. He and his wife Jeanne built and operated the Steamboat Inn, which has catered to steelheaders since the late fifties. He served two terms on the Oregon Fish and Wildlife Commission, was a commissioner on the State

Water Board, and was a member of the National Parks angling advisory group and many other local, state, and federal boards. Frank has worked diligently over the years to protect the North Umpqua; he has received the National Wildlife Federation-Sears Roebuck Foundation Conservationist of the Year Award, the Izaak Walton League Beaver Award for conservation achievement, and the Anders Award for Wild Trout Management. He has been awarded the international Federation of Fly Fishers (FFF) Conservation Award of the Year for his good work in fisheries management and the Conservationist of the Year from the Wild Steelhead Coalition. He has been enshrined in the World Fresh Water Fishing Hall of Fame. In 2011, Frank was appointed by President Sarcozy of France as a "Chevalier" of the Legion of Honor in recognition of France's infinite gratitude and appreciation for his contribution to the United States' decisive role in the liberation of France during WWII. A short time after WWII he was made an Honorary Citizen of Sainte-Marie-du-Mont, the village at Utah Beach in Normandy. He has fished in many places throughout the world, but to him there is only one North Umpqua River.

ED NICHOLSON
To help others heal

IT WAS A NAVY POSTING in the decidedly landlocked state of Idaho that introduced Captain Ed Nicholson to fly fishing.

"I spent my career as an officer in the U.S. Navy," Ed began, "and as you advance through the ranks, you're expected to attend training programs to hone your skills in various specialty areas. In the early eighties, I was selected to take command of a ship. It was felt that anyone in command should have some knowledge of the ship's engineering, and I was slated to attend training in Idaho Falls. I protested that I'd been a chief engineer on a similar ship and really didn't need to attend, but was told that I'd be going. The first thing I did after landing in Idaho Falls was to visit a local fly shop and get outfitted. I'd always enjoyed the outdoors; I had been a bird hunter, and the concept of fly fishing appealed to me. During the three months of my engineering refresher, I had a wonderful training ground for fly fishing, with the Henry's Fork, the Snake, and the Madison in my backyard. I was hooked."

"When you're at sea on a naval ship, your opportunities for fly fishing are pretty limited; you can't very well take a destroyer up onto a bonefish flat! But one of my fellow officers was a fly fisher and a tier, and he showed me how to tie flies during off hours. This helped keep my interest engaged. When I returned to shore duty, there were more opportunities to wet a line. Once I retired, the passion kicked in again. Some of my navy colleagues even formed a little group—the Loyal Order of

Navy Fly Fishers—and we'd do fly-fishing trips to Montana to enjoy all the things that fly fishers enjoy. We still get together now."

It was years after leaving the navy, in the midst of a second career, that Ed *really* reconnected with fly fishing. "In 2005, I had had a major operation and was recuperating in Walter Reed National Military Medical Center," Ed continued. "I was doing a lot of soul searching at the time. I had decided that I'd retire from my private-sector job to spend more time doing things I really enjoyed, like fishing. As I was trying to sort out my future, I couldn't help but notice the men and women around the hospital who had been busted up a lot worse than me. I began to think that some of these guys would love to do something other than sitting around in a hospital room. Maybe they'd like to go fly fishing…and maybe I could take them out. This kernel of thought expanded rapidly. I began thinking about the logistics of taking these vets out fishing, and how you could get guys in their twenties who have lost limbs interested in fly fishing. I contacted Trout Unlimited and they were interested in the idea. I soon found the right person at Walter Reed to help—Colonel William Howard, who was then chief of the occupational therapy clinic. He jumped on the idea. He could see beyond my own goals—to take someone fishing—to the larger therapeutic possibilities that fly fishing could provide. Bill helped us understand how fishing could help put people on the road to recovery. It didn't hurt that he liked to fly fish, too."

It wasn't too long before Ed's kernel of an idea had grown into a full-fledged organization—Project Healing Waters Fly Fishing. Thanks to support from VA hospitals around the country, the Department of Defense, Trout Unlimited, and the Federation of Fly Fishers, Project Healing Waters has grown from one program in Washington, D.C., to one hundred and twenty programs across the United States, Canada, and the United Kingdom.

Ed described the process for attracting new fishing recruits in the early days of the program at Walter Reed. "We started in the winter when you couldn't do much outside, with fly fishing 101 classes, covering all the things you'd cover in any intro class.

When the weather broke in March, we'd go outside to the lawn and teach some casting basics. Our chairperson of the board, Douglas Dear, owns a farm in Virginia with a mile of the Rose River, in addition to several ponds, and we'd go on our ice-breaker fishing outings there. We want to slowly build the individual's comfort level with the sport; you don't want to just take someone with little or no experience out on a river and thrust a rod into their hand. But once the new anglers have the basics down and feel that fish wiggling on that light rod, they want to go back and get another one."

The appeal of fly fishing for returning veterans goes beyond the tug that's so addictive. "There's something magical and beautiful about fly fishing that anyone who's done the sport can identify with," Ed opined. "In my experience, there's something about the experience that strikes an especially resonant chord with people who've been traumatized in war—whether in Iraq or Afghanistan or Vietnam. The chance to commune with nature is part of it. It's hard to stand in a beautiful river and be depressed. Your emotions are immediately boosted. On another level, it's about overcoming your disability. I've seen guys with a missing leg struggle to keep their position in the river, but they maintain their balance and make it back to shore. I believe that they can't help but think 'If I can overcome that, I can overcome other things.' I had one vet (who eventually became a staff member with Project Healing Waters) tell me that he had pretty much given up on his ability to do anything worthwhile, due to his limitations. Over the course of his involvement with fly fishing, he saw he could do other things—and he proved it. I can only imagine being faced with what these folks are dealing with—shattered arms, legs, faces. Somehow fly fishing enables them to progress beyond their disabilities. I've heard many people credit Project Healing Waters with their healing.

"I need to emphasize that so much in the healing process does not happen on the river, but through the friendships that fly fishing generates. It sounds trite, but it's the whole business of developing a family. I see this family growing and engaging all the time. I was at a social event for Project Healing Waters awhile back and noticed a fellow who was obviously enjoying himself, chatting and laughing with other guests. It wasn't someone I knew. A woman tugged on my sleeve. 'See John over there?' she asked. 'Yes,' I said. 'That's my husband John. He's the guy I knew before the war. When he came back, I didn't recognize him. That happy man is what you've given me back.'

"I've been involved with Project Healing Waters for eight years. I don't get a chance to fish as much as I'd like myself. But when I have an experience like this—and see these guys having a better life—I get a great sense of accomplishment."

ED NICHOLSON is president and founder of Project Healing Waters Fly Fishing
(www.projecthealingwaters.org). After graduating from the University of North Carolina in
1964, he received a commission as an ensign in the U.S. Navy. This led to a thirty-year career
that included service in Vietnam, command of a destroyer and a frigate, and two ordnance-
related shore installations, prior to his retirement as a captain in 1994. After retiring from the
navy, Ed worked for ten years for Applied Ordnance Technologies in southern Maryland, the
location of his last duty station. During that time, he worked as a program manager on various
projects and, prior to retiring, was a director, managing offices in three different locations. His
own stay in Walter Reed in 2005 gave him a close look at the returning wounded and was the
genesis for Project Healing Waters. Ed lives in Port Tobacco, Maryland, with his wife, Leslie, his
English setter, Smoke, and a little pointer named Gem.

BRIAN O'KEEFE

Making an impression

FOR A GENERATION OF ANGLERS, Brian O'Keefe has set a high bar for those aspiring to a freewheeling, adventure fishing–oriented (read "fish bum") lifestyle. To think it all started with a nickname and a quiet effort to staunch a *perceived* inclination toward exaggeration!

"When I was in fifth grade, I'd ride my Stingray bike over to Lake Washington from where I lived in Bellevue," Brian began, "and I'd fish for bass. I did pretty well; I'd occasionally bring one or two home, but for the most part, I let them go. My older brother would ask how I did, and I'd say 'I caught a couple nice ones.' I'd go on to tell him exactly where I'd fished, what I used, etc. I should mention that I had a nickname at the time—'Little O'Keefe.' My big brother was a great student, a great athlete, really an all-around good guy. When teachers got me, I think they had great expectations, and I always disappointed them, as I was the kid cracking jokes in the back of the class. I really didn't mind being Little O'Keefe, as I thought my brother was a great guy, too.

"As I kept coming back home with these great stories but no fish, my parents were a little concerned that perhaps my storytelling was getting out of control, and that I was telling tall tales as a way of calling for attention. That Christmas, they got me a Kodak Instamatic, which had recently come on the market. It was a great gift; it was also a little trick—the hope was that I'd use it to take pictures of these 'nice fish' I supposedly caught and either prove or disprove my fish stories. Of course, I didn't know this at the time. Winter passed, and when it warmed up, I took my Stingray, an Arctic Creel holding my camera, a fly rod, and a Bassmaster 5000 down to the lake. I took pictures of the bass I caught on those spring trips, and pretty soon I'd used up my twenty-four exposures. I told my parents that I'd finished the film, and they were shocked. I think they were pretty sure I was taking pictures of pick-up basketball games and anything else I saw. They took the film to an overnight film developer, and when they got the glossies back, there were all these photos of the big bass I'd caught. I was very nonchalant about it; I'd been catching fish like this for a while. My big brother was blown away. The photos had made an impression. When neighbors stopped by to visit, 'Brian's bass pictures' came out and were proudly shared. Suddenly I wasn't 'Little O'Keefe' any more. I had done something cool. I took that Instamatic everywhere after that. I used it all through high school and even took it on my first trip to New Zealand.

"When I was forty, I realized that the attention my snapshots received was the tipping point moment in my life. It was those original bass snapshots that made me what I am. Those pictures foreshadowed my life."

Brian credits his love of adventure—and fly fishing—to his grandfather, Fred W. Johnson. "Grandpa Fred was a forester, and a dry-fly purist. He'd spent time with the RAF [Royal Air Force] in England in World War I, and had learned the chalk stream techniques—cast upstream to feeding fish with a silk line. When he came back to Montana, that was how he fished…and that was how he taught me to fish. We'd walk along the river until we found a rising fish, and then we'd cast upstream.

"In 1951, he and his wife went to New Zealand to fish. This was half a century before trout bums started turning up on the South Island to make videos. He had a map and a detailed diary that he shared. By the age of fourteen, I'd decided that I would go to New Zealand as soon as I could. I mowed lawns, raked leaves, washed cars—did whatever I could do to save money. When I finished high school, I flew to Auckland and stayed in New Zealand for eleven months. I had a backpack, a fiberglass rod with a Pflueger reel, and grandpa's diary, which I used as my road map. I camped, did a few odd jobs now and then, and fished my brains out with dry flies, just like grandpa. The scenery was tremendous, and my Instamatic wasn't quite up to the task. I asked my mother if she could front me one hundred dollars and get me a 35 mm camera. She found a Minolta and sent it along. The stage was set for my addiction to fishing travel. The people I met, the landscapes, the different foods and beverages—I was taken with all the things anglers encounter in a new place. After that adventure, I lived to save and go. I'm more or less doing the same thing today. I think I've made more than sixty trips to Belize and the Bahamas. I've fished in Africa and South America, and throughout Alaska. It hasn't been in a bucket list way. I get interested in a spot because it has interesting landscape or wildlife as much as for the fishing. I often rough it, and can usually find a way to do the trips on the cheap.

"When I'm at fly-fishing shows or doing a presentation at a club, people will come up and say, 'I wish I had your life' or 'You're my hero.' I've had lots of adventures for sure. But I have to remind them that I never had much of a settled life—and never had children. That's a big trade-off. The people who are being good moms and dads are really doing heroic things, as far as I'm concerned. Sometimes I'll get calls or emails out of the blue from high school or college kids, curious about my 'career' and how they might pursue such a lifestyle. I have to bring them down to earth. I tell them there's not much money working around fly fishing, and to get to the point where you can eke out a modest living takes a little luck and lots of perseverance. I also tell the young guys that you really can't blueprint a path to this lifestyle. Your best bet is to do something you're good at and align it with your hobbies. In the long run, you want to hire the fishing guide, not be the fishing guide. Do something traditional and let the fishing follow it.

"I had someone ask me once, 'Have you ever thought about how much money you'd have saved if you didn't travel so much?' I had never thought about it. I feel I have something better than money or things I might have bought; I have a lifetime of great memories."

ABOUT THE ANGLER

BRIAN O'KEEFE has been serious about fly fishing for the past forty years. During the past thirty, cameras have played a significant part in his outdoor lifestyle. His photos have appeared in many leading periodicals, including the *Los Angeles Times*; the *New York Times*; the *Miami Herald*; *USA Today*; and many others. He has had cover shots in *Field & Stream*; *Outdoor Life*; *Fly Fisherman*; *Fly, Rod & Reel*; *Fly Fishing in Salt Waters*; *Outside Magazine*; and *Men's Journal*. In 2010, Brian launched *Catch Magazine* (catchmagazine.net), an online experience that captures the best of fly-fishing film and photography. Brian has traveled to some of the wildest and most remote angling destinations in the world, including Bikini Atoll, the Seychelles, Kenya, Sierra Leone, Tonga, Cuba, and Kashmir. He has also traveled to more accessible locations, such as the Bahamas, Belize, Costa Rica, Nicaragua, Venezuela, Chile, New Zealand, Christmas Island, and more. In many of these locations he again chooses to venture off the beaten path—hiking, floating, sea kayaking, or taking a Zodiac into the backcountry. He has worked in fly-fishing retail, as a guide, as a tackle rep, and as a casting instructor. Brian is also an accomplished fly caster, earning the title of Master Certified Fly Casting Instructor from the Federation of Fly Fishers (FFF). He has placed in, and won, many fly-casting competitions.

FLIP PALLOT
The lifting of the veil

WHILE CREATING AND FILMING *WALKER'S CAY CHRONICLES*—perhaps the greatest fly-fishing programming ever aired—Flip Pallot had the opportunity to visit many of the world's most enticing angling venues. Yet despite his many travels, the home waters still stir his soul.

"I grew up beside the Everglades and came of age in the late 1950s, at a time when fly fishing in salt water was beginning to emerge," Flip began. "Florida was on its way to becoming the epicenter of saltwater fly fishing. It was much later that people began to explore more exotic destinations. By a wonderful accident of birth, I was there at the perfect time to witness the beginnings of the sport, at a time when the resources were unimaginable by today's standards in terms of the number of fish, the quality of the habitat, and the fact that so few people were involved. At any time you decided to go fishing, you had everything to yourself…and if you were interrupted in your solitude, it was by someone you knew. It was the most magic of times in the most magic of places, and I was lucky enough to stumble upon it."

The focus of Flip's fishing has certainly been fly oriented, but he's not averse to other angling methods. Indeed, they've augmented his appreciation of the long rod. "If I hadn't cut my teeth on using other kinds of tackle—plug casting, spinning, offshore, even a piece of string and a hook tied to my toe—I don't think I'd enjoy fly fishing as much as I do," he continued. "I'd have nothing to compare it to in terms

LEFT
The Everglades—where Flip Pallot cut his fly-fishing teeth.

of what makes it special and wouldn't have appreciated all the skill it demands…
and probably would not have risen to the same levels of proficiency that I targeted.
While I still enjoy those other kinds of tackle, fly fishing remains fresh by its comparisons to other angling styles."

Though fly fishing has been a livelihood for Flip—first as a guide and later as an
on-screen personality—it has seldom seemed like work. "That moment when I put
my hand on the piling and push away from the dock, I'm free from everything else
that's happening on the planet," he said. "That includes cell phones, computers, red
lights, and the hostility and competition of daily life; all that fades away as I push
off. Fly fishing is so deeply identified with that moment of release, the feeling of a
veil or mantle lifting. All of its attendant sounds and smells—the sounds and smells
of the flats or the river—replace everyday sounds and smells. For fly anglers, these
moments are among the happiest in our lives. The moment we push away from the
dock, we're no longer thinking about melanoma or board meetings. We're focused
on one mission, dropping out…if only for a day."

Flip Pallot is a man of generous spirit, but not one who suffers fools lightly, especially on the bow of his skiff. "These days, if you're on the deck of my boat, it's
because I want you there. When I guided it was a little different. I'd only take one
person at a time. Something that made it interesting—and still makes it interesting—is trying to see my world through my companion's eyes. I've been at it so long,
have seen so much. It's fascinating to envision another person's view of what's happening around them. If they miss seeing the bald eagle on its nest, I notice that they
missed the eagle. If they miss the banded water snake, I notice that. That person's
stock doesn't go down in these cases; I'm just curious. Some people are there for the
total experience. Others are there only to fish. Others only want to catch a particular
kind of fish. I like to observe and chronicle, but I don't judge.

"I received some great insights when I recently donated a trip to Casting for Recovery
(a nonprofit group that provides an opportunity for women with breast cancer to

gather in a natural setting and learn the sport of fly fishing). The woman who came on the trip had been through hell with her treatments; the fact that she could even present herself was impressive. She was interested in the fishing, but she missed absolutely nothing. It wasn't the greatest fishing day, but it was a day when I got to see more of my world through her eyes than I have in the prior twelve trips. It was a really exciting day for me in terms of getting a view into what's going on between the ears of the other person in the boat."

Many memorable fly-fishing experiences are defined by great fish landed or great fish lost. One of Flip's defining moments involves a bit of photography. "It was in the early to mid-sixties, and I was fishing in the Everglades a lot—and was getting a reputation for knowing the area. I had met Lefty Kreh about that time and he wanted to fish there, so it came about that I would take him out. We headed into the back-country, and way back there we came upon a flock of flamingos on this enormous, shallow flat. I'd come upon them before; they were resident. Lefty asked, 'Are those flamingos?' and I said yes. 'Can we pole up?' he asked. As I pushed us toward the birds, he produced out of his plunder a single-lens reflex camera with a 400 mm lens and a gun-stock mount. He began photographing the flamingos, using black-and-white film. As we poled closer, we could see that there were scores of redfish among their legs, chasing the critters the flamingos were stirring up. Lefty took at least one hundred pictures before even picking up his fly rod. This made a tremendous impression on me. Any other angler would've thought about the camera but would've picked up the fly rod instead. It amazed me that he was more interested in preserving the memory on film instead of catching redfish. He did eventually pick up the rod and land some fish. It was very apparent that he was indeed the fly-rod luminary that I'd heard he was.

"He has since become a tremendous part of my life, and we've enjoyed a long friendship. Everything he's shared with me since has helped point me in the right direction. From a humble fishing trip, a life experience can sprout."

ABOUT THE ANGLER

FLIP PALLOT was born and raised in the middle of a triangle smack between Biscayne Bay, the Florida Everglades, and the Florida Keys, and has lived in the Sunshine State for most of his life. After four years as a linguist for the U.S. Army and a career in banking that lasted "way too long," Flip began guiding anglers in south Florida. Hurricane Andrew destroyed his home and gear, and although this disaster ended his guiding career, it helped launch his TV career. After guest appearances on ABC's *American Sportsman* and the *Outdoor Life* series, he hosted *Saltwater Angler*, which aired for two years on TBS. The *Walker's Cay Chronicles* program was born soon after and aired original programming for sixteen seasons on ESPN. Flip also spent a few seasons with Glenn Lau filming *Quest for Adventure*, which aired on OLN, and hosted *Fishing the Keys* on the Versus network. He's now hosting *Ford's Fishing Frontiers*, airing weekends on the Outdoor Channel. Flip has written several books, including *Mangroves, Memories and Magic* and a biography of Lefty Kreh called *All The Best*. The book has a companion two-DVD set entitled *All the Best: A Conversation with Flip Pallot and Lefty Kreh*. Flip splits his time between Mims and Yankeetown, Florida, with summers in Idaho chasing trout with his best fishing buddy (and wife), Diane.

NICK PRICE
You never stop learning

SINCE 1977, Nick Price has earned his living (and legions of fans) playing golf. But he'll readily admit that his *real* passion is fly fishing.

"My dad was a huge fisherman," Nick recalled, "and so were my brothers. Nearly all of our holidays were spent as fishing trips. When we lived in Durban, we'd head to the Drakensberg Mountains and stay in cottages close to all the streams there. Brown and rainbow trout had been introduced to some of the rivers. When I was a toddler, my father would take my two older brothers fly fishing downstream, and I'd be left by the car with my mother while the boys went off to fish. I vividly remember complaining that I wanted to go fishing. My dad had a couple trout rods, and he ended up tying nine feet of leader material to the top eye of one of the rods and attached a fly to the end. I found a log that went over the stream by our camp, and I sat for hours on that log working the fly while he and the older boys went off on their own. Eventually, I caught a small rainbow, and they all came back empty-handed. I was three and a half.

"When I was six or seven, my dad taught me how to throw a fly rod. By this time, we'd moved to Rhodesia. The eastern highlands of Rhodesia, like the Drakensbergs, had streams where trout had been introduced. The streams were very small, and when you learn to fish on such small streams, you're very close to the fish. Many times you can see them and have to stalk them. This was how I got the taste of fly fishing. Once you get competent enough with your casting and fly presentation, it's all about the hunt. That's why sight casting to fish will always be the most exciting form of fly fishing for me."

Given Nick's love of sight fishing, it's no surprise that bonefish are a favorite quarry. "I've really gravitated to flats fishing," Nick continued. "I've got a flats boat, and I more often than not fish with my wife, Sue. She can throw a fly rod fairly well, but mostly uses spinning tackle. I have always loved to pole the flats, as you see so much more being elevated and constantly learn the habits of bonefish. Sue can pole pretty well, too, but only downwind and frequently puts me on fish. Sometimes I'll anchor up on a flat on an incoming tide and wade near a slough, hoping to intercept the fish as they're coming in. I'd rather look for bigger fish than focus on numbers, and you're more likely to find the big guys on the edge, closer to the deep water, rather than in the middle of the flat. There are three parts of bonefishing that define the experience for me. The first is seeing the fish; the second is getting into position to make the cast; the third is when the fish turns on the fly and takes it. The first run is always a thrill, but as soon as you get that fish in and release it, you're looking for the next one. Andros Island is one of my favorite places to chase bonefish. I've had wonderful days at Joulters' Cays (north of Andros) and on the western side of the island, but I have also fished sporadically in the Florida Keys. There aren't as many fish in the Keys, but they are generally bigger than the Bahamian fish and harder to catch. In three or four days of fishing, you have a good chance of seeing a number of double-digit-weight fish, but in order to catch them, you have to be a very proficient caster." (Nick has landed several fish in that class.)

Perhaps it's the outdoor setting, pitting man against natural obstacles (be they finicky trout or gaping bunkers). Perhaps it's the similitude of the swinging and casting motion—the fact that the ball/fly goes farther with an easy stroke that allows the club/rod to do the work. Whatever the reason, many PGA pros—including Jack Nicklaus, Mark O'Meara, Padraig Harrington, Nick Faldo, Davis Love III, Justin

Leonard, David Duval, and Paul Azinger—spend many of their off-fairway hours with a fly rod in hand. When asked about the shared passions of golf and fly fishing, Nick had several interesting observations. "At heart, most golfers are outdoorsmen. They appreciate anything that takes them out into the fresh air—be it hunting or fly fishing. There's also the role the field of play has in the experience. You can put two golf courses next to each other, and each course can be completely different...and they can demand that you play them differently to have success. The same can be said of two rivers, or the difference between fishing a clear stream or being on a flat for bonefish or permit. Each requires different techniques to be successful.

"I think the most telling similarity between golf and fly fishing is that with both sports, you're constantly learning, constantly trying to improve your methodology. Just because you played golf well one day doesn't mean you'll play well the next. I've been playing golf professionally for thirty-five years, and I often find myself saying, 'Why didn't I figure out what I'm working on now back in my twenties?' The same is true of fishing. If you ever think you know everything about fishing, you're in deep trouble. The fish behave differently wherever you are, and you need to try to stay a step ahead of them. That's what fascinates me about fly fishing. You never stop learning, and that's what gets me really excited every day I go fishing.

"My favorite time to play golf is late afternoon, as the sun is setting. For a man to head out and play nine holes with his son or daughter or wife, enjoying the last light—that's the essence of the game. Fishing at that time is also special. If my wife and I are going out on the flats, we'll be on the boat by nine and fish through lunch until three or four. Then we'll go offshore a bit and drop a bait down and fish for grouper and snapper for the barbecue and watch the sun go down. Sitting out there, that's fishing nirvana."

ABOUT THE ANGLER

NICK PRICE is a professional golfer who has tallied eighteen PGA Tour victories and twenty-four international wins since turning pro in 1977. In 1994, he enjoyed one of golf's greatest seasons, winning six tourneys, including the British Open and the PGA Championship; he was named PGA Tour Player of the Year in both 1993 and 1994. He is commonly regarded as one of the kindest and most personable people in the game and has received the Bob Jones Award for distinguished sportsmanship in golf. Nick began collaborating on golf-course designs in the early nineties and has developed courses in the United States, Caribbean, United Kingdom, and South Africa through his company, Nick Price Golf Course Design. Since joining the Champions Tour in 2007, he has won three tourneys. Nick was inducted into the World Golf Hall of Fame in 2003. He lives in Florida with his wife, Sue, and has three children—Gregory, Robyn Frances, and Kimberly Rae...and he hopes to fish in Iceland, Russia's Kola Peninsula, and other adventurous spots around the world once he's hung up his clubs.

TOM ROSENBAUER

It's part of my DNA

TOM ROSENBAUER'S INTRODUCTION TO FISHING might have horrified the stereotypical tweed-jacketed, eastern-establishment fly angler of yesteryear. "My dad was a worm fisherman, and that's how I got started," he recalled. "We fished for panfish and catfish, and I took to it. When my dad went off into golf—back in the sixties, before it was cool—I stayed with fishing. We lived in Rochester, along the south shore of Lake Ontario, and I'd ride my bike to places to fish for white perch, bass; I even remember snagging carp with treble hooks. Somewhere around age ten or eleven, I decided that fly fishing looked interesting. I must have seen pictures in a sporting catalog or Field & Stream. Before I ever fly fished, I bought a fly-tying kit and began tying flies. I wish I had saved some of my early ties; I'm sure they were a disaster.

"My dad had an old steel fly rod with an automatic reel and an old silk level line lay- ing around the house, and I began taking it to a little pond near my house that had small largemouth bass, six inches to ten inches. It was all sight fishing; it was great for experimenting with the flies I had tied. I remember pretending that the bass were trout. A guy on my paper route told me about a tiny stream that ran through a local golf course that had wild brook trout. When I checked it out, I found brookies spawning all through its upper reaches. I played around catching them on dry flies and scuds. By this time, I was really taken with fly fishing and got out every book in the local library that I could find on the topic—all two or three of them! Learning to cast by myself with no videos or fly-fishing schools was very frustrating. I didn't know anyone who could cast, so I was on my own. Despite hours on the lawn, it took me years to figure it out."

Fortunately, help was on the way. "When I was fourteen, I met a man named Carl Coleman," Tom continued. "He worked for Kodak, and he ran a little fly shop out of his house. He was considered the guru for the streams around Rochester, and he took me under his wing; I think I was the son that he never had. He taught me more about fly tying, and started having me tie Catskill-style dry flies for his shop. I tied for Carl all through high school and made enough money to buy three or four bamboo rods. I didn't really have anywhere else I could spend my money! Around the same time, I had a buddy from Boy Scouts who got a car, and we started taking road trips to fish the famous streams of the Adirondacks, the Catskills, and Pennsylvania. We learned together and did a lot of laughing. Sometimes he'd hide on the bank, smoke dope, and throw pebbles to imitate rising fish. It was my goal to be a fisheries biologist, and I went to SUNY College of Environmental Science and Forestry to pursue a fisheries major. I fished a lot through college, though most of my friends found other things besides trout to chase. To make ends meet, I taught some fly-tying classes, worked for a fly shop in Syracuse and at a mail-order fly-tying materials house. I got to know the business of fly fishing early on."

Tom seems to have been fated to work in the fly-fishing industry, despite his attempts to do otherwise. "When I graduated with my fisheries degree, I realized that to do what I wanted to do, I'd need a master's degree…except I didn't have any money," he explained. "I answered an ad for a clerk at the Orvis retail store in Manchester, Vermont. I'd hoped to save enough money to go back to grad school, but at six thousand dollars a year, there wasn't enough. I didn't love working retail, but luckily other things opened up. Orvis needed someone to run the fly-tying materials program, and I did that. I started doing some writing and editing of marketing materials, and this led to my working on the catalog, then other roles in public relations, merchandising, and advertising. Eventually I ran product development for fly fishing. Now I have myself a comfortable spot (as marketing director for Orvis Rod and Tackle) where I can do a mix of PR, marketing, and social media."

Orvis is one of the oldest and perhaps best-known brands in the fly-fishing world, and perversely enough, that has posed Tom one of his greater challenges as the company's public fishing face. "Many people—especially in the western United States—have a preconception of Orvis as a stodgy and stuffy company. They see us as big corporate fly fishing. That's not the reality at all. Because the company is privately held, we don't have a corporate culture—at least not in the fly-fishing area. Everybody here fly fishes, and they're good. To sit in the office with a dozen people who are so passionate about fishing and hunting—it's hard to match. We fish and hunt before work, during our lunch hour, and after work; working at Orvis is living the dream!"

Tom's long career at Orvis comprises only a portion of his contributions to fly fishing. He's also authored many books and articles over the years. "I had been editing the *Orvis News*, which had a circulation of four hundred thousand, making it the world's biggest fly-fishing publication," he explained. "I ran into Nick Lyons (then of Lyons Press) at a Trout Unlimited event. He mentioned that he had noticed my writing, and he asked me to do a book. That led to another and another. Nick is still a good friend. In fact, I'm working with him on a new title." (As of this writing, Tom has penned eleven fly-fishing titles, all still in print.)

Work and fly fishing have been closely intertwined in Tom's life, but that has hardly diminished his zeal for a day on the water—almost any kind of fishing water. "Everything gets me excited," Tom enthused. "I have wild trout in my backyard. If it's August and clear and cool and I know there's going to be a good Trico hatch, I can't sleep the night before. If I'm on a lake and there are pumpkinseed under a dock, I can't resist trying to catch them. I love going offshore for anything in the tuna family—bonito, skipjacks, albacore. I love being out on the open water with pods of whales and dolphins. A few years back, we were finding juvenile bluefin tuna just a mile off the coast of Rhode Island. Conditions hardly ever come together to see this happen; it was phenomenal. It's worse than permit fishing in terms of actually hooking them, but it's a thrill when you do."

"People who take up the sport in midlife might have Howell Raines–style epiphanies," Tom added. "Having done it forever, it's just part of my DNA. But it's always new and always changing. I can't get tired of it."

ABOUT THE ANGLER

TOM ROSENBAUER, host of the Orvis fly-fishing podcasts, has been with the Orvis Company for more than thirty years, and while there, has been a fishing-school instructor, copywriter, public relations director, merchandise manager, and editor of the *Orvis News* for ten years. He is currently marketing director for Orvis Rod and Tackle. As merchandise manag-

er, web merchandiser, and catalog director, Tom has guided the titles under his direction to win numerous gold medals in the Annual Catalog Age Awards. Tom has been a fly fisher for more than thirty-five years and was a commercial fly tier by age fourteen. He has fished extensively across North America and has also fished on Christmas Island, the Bahamas, in Kamchatka, and on the fabled English chalk streams. He is credited with bringing Beadhead flies to North America, and is the inventor of the Big Eye hook, Magnetic Net retriever, and tungsten beads for fly tying. Tom has eleven fly-fishing books in print, including *The Orvis Fly-Fishing Guide*; *Reading Trout Streams*; *Prospecting for Trout*; *Casting Illusions*; *Fly Fishing in America*; *Approach and Presentation*; *Trout Foods and Their Imitations*; *Nymphing Techniques*; *Leaders, Knots, and Tippets*; *The Orvis Guide to Dry-Fly Techniques*; and *The Orvis Fly-Tying Guide*, which won a 2001 National Outdoor Book Award. He has also been published in *Field & Stream*, *Outdoor Life*, *Catalog Age*, *Fly Fisherman*, *Gray's Sporting Journal*, *Sporting Classics*, *Fly Rod & Reel*, *Audubon*, and others. In 2011, he received *Fly Rod & Reel* magazine's Angler of the Year award.

DAVE ROSGEN
A laboratory for the senses

"I GREW UP FISHING QUARTZ AND SKULL CREEK, tributaries to the North Fork Clearwater River in Idaho," Dave Rosgen began. "I had fished these streams in the 1950s when you had to pack in by horseback. I didn't fish there while I was in high school and college. After graduation, I went to work for the forest service in the very ranger district these streams were located. By that time roads had been built along the creeks for logging operations that were clear-cutting up in the creeks' headwaters. I had been looking forward to fishing those great cutthroat streams upon my return, but instead I was left with the vision of impaired waters. Thanks to erosion from the clear-cutting, the habitat had shifted from a substrate of cobble and gravel with scattered boulders to large boulders dominated by sand invasion. To make matters worse, on my first fishing outing I was skunked! The forest service didn't have money to fix the problem. I was upset with the state of these rivers, and I wanted to fix them."

Thus began Dave Rosgen's long career restoring, reinvigorating, and at times reimagining abused rivers. His early hydrology work was conducted as a forest service employee, remediating streams impacted by timber harvest in the 1960s. In 1984, he formed Wildland Hydrology Consultants, and has been doing watershed assessment and river restoration ever since. He has worked on hundreds of rivers, including

Nevada Creek in Montana, the Little Snake River in Wyoming, the Big Thompson River, Blue River, and one of his crowning achievements, Rio Blanco, in Colorado.

"When I first visited Rio Blanco in 1987, it seemed like the valley of the ranch where it flows, El Rancho Pinoso, was one big gravel bar," Dave continued. "The Blanco was anywhere from 350 to 500 feet wide and just inches deep, when the river bed should be 50 or 60 feet wide. You had a system that had no hope to be anything but a very poor fishery…though with a little help, the stream could provide great fish habitat." To create habitat that would support trout in the valley reaches of Rio Blanco, it was necessary to reshape the river enough to stem erosion and create deeper pockets of water to provide shelter for fish. Before he could begin to create a blueprint to implement the necessary changes, Dave needed to find a river in the region that had a similar flow regime, and hence was naturally stable. Once such a model was found—the East Fork of the San Juan in an adjoining valley—he set to work, hauling in boulders and portions of old trees to rejuvenate the Blanco's banks and direct its waters toward a more defined channel. "My goal was to develop a naturally meandering stream that has a close connection to the surrounding riparian environs. In the past, methods included rock rip rap, gabion baskets, concrete, and even junked cars to shore up stream banks. That doesn't exactly give the river a natural feel."

One of the main challenges Dave faced on Rio Blanco was filtering out the massive amounts of sediment that have carried down from the mountains during spring runoff. If sediment was not diverted, the stream bed would be clogged, and water would flow outside of the primary channel. Rosgen and his team constructed a tube to divert cobble, gravel, and sand away from the river channel; water flows through, and sediment is routed to a holding area that can be periodically emptied out. The excess gravel is used to supplement roads and trails around El Rancho Pinoso. Thanks to Dave Rosgen's efforts, there are three miles of Rio Blanco that hold a healthy population of reintroduced rainbows.

Fly fishing was one of the inspirations for Dave's work, and each day continues to inform it. "Fly fishing not only fully engrosses one's senses but challenges the conscious soul," he ventured. "It is the one sport you have to work at that doesn't feel like work. It's an activity that can engulf one so deeply and thoroughly as to camouflage the stresses and worries of the day. Fly fishing creates a laboratory for the study of the physical and biological system while saturating the soul with a sense of wonder and appreciation of one's surroundings. My years of fly fishing have provided a better understanding of habitat and where fish hold, what they eat and at what part of the river profile they feed, and how it varies by season, by stage, and by time of day. The focus necessary for fly fishing provides insight into the flow hydraulics and resistance that creates the habitat diversity within the water column.

"Fly fishing has also created an opportunity for me to improve the biological function of my restoration projects by offsetting the limiting factors of habitat, creating diversity, and knowing the ultimate biological potential. The creation of in-stream holding cover with native materials; spawning and rearing habitat; aquatic and terrestrial 'food plots'; and a riparian corridor that provides overhead cover, shade, and terrestrial insects are all on the design sheets. Such designs are generated as a result of many years of fly fishing and study with fisheries biologists who also continue to contribute their understanding to my education over the years. The first requirement for any student in the study of hydrology, geomorphology, fisheries, and civil engineering should be 'fly fishing 101,' for such study would develop an understanding of values lost if the habitat is not treated appropriately and a sense of duty to protect and enhance the physical and biological system to perpetuate the fly-fishing experience for now and for future generations. Fly fishing also helps develop a 'feel' for rivers beyond the mathematical expressions of the science."

Some of Dave's restoration projects can take years from inception to completion. There are days, no doubt, when he must feel that he is, quite literally, fighting against an unrelenting current. But when a restoration comes to fruition, the sense of fulfillment is tremendous. "I get the greatest satisfaction from catching trout in the habitat I've designed," Dave said. "I 'test' fish the habitat of my projects and at the end of the day, I look upstream and recall what was versus what is. I'm so appreciative of having had the opportunity to create sustainable fisheries and self-maintaining river systems.

"Each year, I take my two sons to either the Blue River or the Little Snake River to fly fish my projects. It makes me so happy to hear their war whoops after hooking a big one!"

ABOUT THE ANGLER

DAVE ROSGEN operates Wildland Hydrology Consultants (www.wildlandhydrology.com), which restores rivers and offers classes based on his methods. He has published two books highlighting his work—*Applied River Morphology* and *Watershed Assessment for River Stability and Sediment Supply*. Dave has been widely recognized for his work, including an Outstanding Achievement Award from the U.S. Environmental Protection Agency in 1993, recognition in *National Geographic*'s special "Water Issue" in 1993, the Leopold Conservation Award from the Federation of Fly Fishers in 2001, and recognition as an innovator of the year in science by *Time* magazine in 2004. He resides in Fort Collins, Colorado.

ROBERT RUBIN
The camaraderie runs deep

MUCH OF ROBERT RUBIN'S LONG CAREER in the financial industry has
unfolded in the granite-ribbed canyons of Manhattan. Yet it's the broad meadows of
Montana and the white sand flats of the Bahamas that command his attention whenever time permits. "I love to get out to the spring creeks in the Ruby River Valley,
O'Dell Creek near Ennis, Nelson's Spring Creek by Livingston, the Boulder River
near Big Timber and Slough Creek in Yellowstone National Park, up by Meadows
Three and Four," Robert began. "I also love bonefishing. My two favorite Bahamian
destinations are North Riding Point on Grand Bahama Island and Flamingo Key
on the west side of Andros Island. Over the last twenty-five years, I must have been
down there one hundred times, mostly quick two-day trips."

The delicacy of spring creek fishing has great appeal to Robert. "These waters are
very technical," he continued. "The streams are intimate, the water is flat and very
clear, and there tend to be many small currents, which make presentation challenging. You have to get the fly—often a very small one—to just the right place. And you
have to be very careful, as the trout are particularly sensitive. A cast that's too long, a
fly that drags across the water, even too heavy a footfall on the bank can spook them,
and you may as well move to a different spot. I like to use very light rods, which
make for a delicate presentation. I had one very fine day last summer on a spring
creek near Dillon, using a one-weight. In the course of the day, I hooked maybe ten

fish over twenty inches. I could only land four of the fish. When I switched to a four-weight, it was a little easier to get the big fish to hand."

One of the mantras many fly-casting instructors try to impart to their acolytes is "let the rod do the work." This is not always easy when the pressure is on, though perhaps it may be most important at these times, as Robert discovered. "There's a stretch on another little spring creek in the Dillon area that's long and flat, and the water is very thin," he shared. "It doesn't look like great fish habitat, but for whatever reason, there are quite a few fish there. I came upon this stretch one time, and across from me, near a piece of the bank that jutted out into the river, a big rainbow was slowly feeding. It didn't move at all, just kept rising to the bugs that were floating by. I was using a two-weight and a size 20 fly. I kept casting to the fish, but was missing the mark. If I'd cast too far, I would've hit the bank and the drag of the leader would've put the fish down. Fortunately, I didn't do that. I realized that I was putting too much into the cast. I took a deep breath, slowed down my cast, and smoothed out the rhythm. Within a few casts, I managed to get the fly right into the fish's feeding lane, and the trout finally took it—a twenty-one-inch rainbow. It was very exciting to hook a fish like that in such thin water."

Fishing tiny dries to finicky trout can make you reevaluate your perspective: Am I imitating the right bug? Is my pattern the right size? Is the drift right? At the end of the day, however, it's the trout's perspective that matters most. "Some years ago I was fishing with a guide on Nelson's Spring Creek," Robert recalled. "There was a big fish rising in a microcurrent below some subsurface structure, just sipping and sipping. I thought that most of the casts were pretty good, but apparently the fish thought otherwise. After a few more casts, the guide stopped me and said, 'You've had a lot of good casts in there. None of the bad casts have been so bad as to spook the fish. To you all the good casts look the same. But to the fish, they all look different. There may be some drag you don't see, maybe the fly is coming at him at a funny angle.' I resumed casting. On the twenty-second cast, the fish took the fly."

Something must have been different, though that cast looked just like the others to me."

As any financier or politician knows, assembling a winning deal requires both careful planning and smooth execution. Yet there are times when intangibles arise that even the most painstaking situation analysis cannot anticipate. Robert recalled one such incident. "I was fishing out of North Riding Point on Grand Bahama Island. I'd had a great morning, finding a twelve-pound bonefish. After that, we had a dry period where we didn't see anything. Suddenly, a school of about ten fish—all in the twelve-pound range—appeared. Neither the guide nor I had ever seen a school of such large fish, as big bones tend to be solitary. They were moving very slowly. The guide got the boat into position, and I got ready to cast. It would've been easy for me to screw the cast up, but this one landed right. I was all ready for the take—ready to strip set—and just as the bones started moving toward the fly, a little jack burst into the school from underneath in pursuit of the fly. All the bonefish spooked. I would've dove into the water and strangled that jack if I could have!"

Have the patience, tenacity, instinct, and sense of timing fostered in fly fishing helped inform Robert Rubin's political and business acumen? "I would have to say no," Robert replied after a moment's reflection. "But what's struck me is that when I go into a meeting and find that someone on the other side of the table fly fishes, there's a camaraderie that's quickly established. You realize that you both care enormously about something outside of the room. It may not have anything to do with the issue you're meeting about, but it connects you."

And making a good connection can be an excellent starting point for drafting a resolution that's equitable to all parties.

ABOUT THE ANGLER

ROBERT E. RUBIN served as the seventieth Secretary of the Treasury from January 10, 1995, until July 2, 1999. He joined the Clinton administration in 1993, and served as assistant to the president on economic policy and as the first director of the National Economic Council. He joined the Goldman Sachs Group, Inc., in 1966 and served as cochair from 1990 to 1992. From 1999 to 2009, Robert served as a member of the board of directors at Citigroup and as a senior advisor to the company. In 2010, he joined Centerview Partners as counselor of the firm. Robert is chair of the board of the Local Initiatives Support Corporation (LISC), the nation's leading community development support organization. He serves on the board of trustees of Mount Sinai Medical Center and is a member of the Harvard Corporation. In June 2007, he was named cochair of the Council on Foreign Relations. In 2005, Robert was one of the founders of the Hamilton Project, an economic policy project housed at the Brookings Institution that offers a strategic vision and innovative policy proposals on how to create a growing economy that benefits more Americans. He is author of *In An Uncertain World: Tough Choices from Wall Street to Washington* (Random House, 2003, with Jacob Weisberg), a *New York Times* best seller and one of *Business Week*'s ten best business books of the year. Robert graduated summa cum laude from Harvard College in 1960 with an A.B. in economics. He received an L.L.B. from Yale Law School in 1964 and attended the London School of Economics. He has received honorary degrees from Harvard, Yale, Columbia, and other universities.

ROBERT SWAN

It's about how you fish

"WHEN I WAS A YOUNG BOY, I remember being in my parents' car and hearing some violin music come on the radio," Robert Swan recalled. "Had I been walking, I would've stopped in my tracks—the sound was so beautiful, so compelling. I soon started playing violin, and later transitioned to viola. To become truly excellent on the instrument, you have to make sacrifices. Countless hours are spent in drudgery, learning where the notes go, how to use the bow to produce the right sounds. It's lots of work before you can begin to achieve the level of knowing that begins to approach a sort of grace. Music lovers attending a chamber music concert see the musicians on stage in their white ties and tails; it all looks rather easy and graceful, but you only get to the point where it looks that way by lots of hard work.

"When the movie version of *A River Runs Through It* came out, I heard many people say similar things about the shadow-casting scenes, that it was beautiful and graceful. Yet as an angler, I knew that one doesn't start out like that." (If you haven't guessed it, that wasn't Brad Pitt unfurling those ninety-foot casts. Director Robert Redford employed several "casting doubles" in the making of the film, including Jason Borger, John Dietsch, and Jerry Siem, though Jason has pointed out that all the principal actors could fly cast.)

"When you play music professionally, you've done your hard work—trained your fingers to land on that same millimeter of the fingerboard each time. Once you get that work done, you'd think that the music you create is the payoff. Often it is, but there's something beyond that. Music enables you to express complex emotions, beyond just happy and sad. It can get me to the source of those feelings. It gives a glimpse of something deeper and different where emotions aren't so touched by routine day-to-day contexts. When this happens, one's sense of time changes. Time seems to stall. At times when I have a difficult passage to play, I use a little trick where I imagine that I'm in a slower world and play those fast notes in the slower world.

"I see a clear parallel here with fly fishing. When you're struggling to learn how to cast and to understand the dynamics of a river, you might catch a fish. You'll revel in that, though on some level you recognize it as a 'gift' fish. The real satisfaction comes when you have a greater understanding of what's going on and are presented with situations where you have to make a demanding cast to have a shot at the fish. You don't always make it, but it's a great feeling when you do. To get to that point, you have to endure a lot of bad casts. If you practice enough though, you'll come out on the other end and be able to cast well. The fish may be the payoff, but the grace of casting is a big part of the game for me.

"Every day in the spring and summer I go out into my front yard and cast for fifteen minutes working on loop control. I remember once asking this guide/casting guru how long I'd have to keep looking over my shoulder at my back cast. The answer was, 'For the rest of your life, Bob.'"

Given the exacting demands of his professional life, some of Bob's friends have wondered at his choice of recreation. "Someone challenged me awhile back," he recalled. "'Why take up fly fishing? You have to be precise and deal with more of that 'fine motor sh—. Why not go for a bike ride?' For me, a big part of it is the challenge of learning and getting better at something that's difficult. Thus, through this process fly fishing can give each of us a glimpse of who we are.

"I remember my first encounter with fly fishing, when I was a boy in Connecticut. I was wading along a creek with my blue Garcia/Conolon rod and Mitchell 300 reel. I got to a larger pool, and there in front of a big white house was a guy wearing a funky little hat and a vest, and he was carrying a bamboo rod. He seemed all gussied up. We got to chatting and he offered, 'I prefer to fly fish.' I didn't know what to think about that at the time, but now I've sort of become that guy but without the funky hat. Like that guy in front of his house, I'm snobby about it; that's the way I like to fish, whether it's for trout in the Rockies or bluegill at a local lake. Years later I was fishing out in Montana. The guide I fished with had posted a wonderful saying on the cabin wall where I'd stay: 'It's not about the fish you caught; it's about how you caught the fish.' To my way of thinking, this axiom applies to many avenues beyond fishing. It says 'You can conduct your life in a responsible, principled way.'

"Say you're on a stream in late August. You can see some trout down in a deep hole, but the water temperature is seventy-plus degrees. You could drift a nymph in front of them, and they'll probably take it. But the fish may die fighting because of the heat. So don't fish! It's not about the fish you caught; it's about the respect that you have for the fish around you. If you have respect for your quarry, it's likely to spill over into other things in your life. If you respect the water, you're less likely to throw a cigarette butt on the sidewalk."

ABOUT THE ANGLER

ROBERT SWAN was appointed to the viola section of the Chicago Symphony Orchestra by Sir Georg Solti in 1972. A native of Connecticut, Robert studied viola with David Dawson at Indiana University, where he earned bachelor's and master's degrees as well as a performer's certificate. While at Indiana, he studied chamber music with William Primrose, Josef Gingold, György Sebök, and Menahem Pressler. Principal viola of Chicago's Music of the Baroque and a founding member of the Evanston Chamber Ensemble, Robert also has appeared as guest artist with the Fine Arts Quartet, the Vermeer Quartet, the Chicago Chamber Musicians, and the Rembrandt Chamber Players. From 1972 until 1980, he was professor of viola at Northwestern University, and he also served as violist of the Eckstein String Quartet. He recently retired from the CSO and spends most of his time in Michigan enjoying a traffic-free life and more fishing.

ROBERT TOMES

The thrill that never stops giving

ROBERT TOMES WAS CATAPULTED INTO FLY FISHING at the young age of fourteen by a passing comment from his mother: "I think there's a fishing store opening in downtown Wilmette."

"I went down to the storefront not long after," Robert recalled. "We didn't live far from downtown or Lake Michigan (along the North Shore of Chicago), and I already had the fishing bug pretty bad, riding my bike down to the waterfront after school with friends to catch perch, bluegill, carp—occasionally a steelhead or salmon—with our spinning rods. The windows of the storefront were still covered in newspapers, including a story on trout fishing from the *New York Times*. I knocked on the door and a kindly, gray-bearded man in a tattersall shirt and tweed jacket—the epitome of a fly angler—answered the door. His name was Andy Burrows and the store was called The Trout & Grouse. I told him I wanted to help him out; to my surprise, he let me hang around the store and eventually hired me. I still remember vividly a time before Christmas when the first big order of Orvis gear arrived. We sat there opening boxes of rods, reels, and flies. I'd read a lot about fly fishing but didn't have much hands-on experience. This was like the best Christmas ever, even though it wasn't my gear.

"There were other factors that converged at this time to help insure that fly fishing would be a major part of my life. My father, who was a corporate executive, saw my intense interest in the sport. He also recognized that there were a lot of bad things teenagers could get into (it was the seventies after all), and that fishing might help keep me on the straight and narrow. I don't think my dad ever fully understood the appeal of fly fishing, but he fostered my interest, buying me tackle and taking me on father and son fishing trips up north in Wisconsin. Likewise, the clientele of The Trout & Grouse—along with Andy Burrows—acted as my mentors. By age sixteen, I was teaching fly tying and casting, but I didn't have the life experience of my well-traveled customers. Several took me under their wing and brought me along on their adventures, first in the Midwest, then on to Florida and Montana. These men established a theme of sharing one's skills and experience that's stuck with me. I've always tried to pass along what knowledge I've gained freely, rather than trying to hoard it."

Robert is passionate when describing how important a role fly fishing has played in his existence. "It has been the nexus, the very core connection to so many strings in my life for as long as I can remember," he offered. "It helped define me in my adolescent years and broadened the scope of my life experience at an early age beyond what many people are exposed to much later in life; it complemented my first career (in the paper business) and fueled my second career as a professional fly-fishing writer and speaker. Lastly, it has served as an entrée for me to make lasting friendships with a vast network of like-minded people at home and around the world, in such varied and exotic destinations as New Zealand, South Africa, Japan, Thailand, British Columbia, Costa Rica, and Patagonia. I consistently find that people who share a love for fly fishing are the people I want to be around—people who enjoy quiet pursuits, like the challenge of learning, and who appreciate results that require an investment in time and skills.

"Almost everything in my life connects back to fly fishing. Maybe it's cliché but it's like a religion; when I do it, it gives me a sense of well-being, a focus. It clears my head and helps me figure things out."

Robert has had the good fortune to pursue a host of fresh- and saltwater species, and enjoys them all. He may be best known for showing the world that muskies— the totem sport fish of the Midwest North Woods—could be effectively pursued with a fly rod. He explained the appeal. "In northern Wisconsin and Minnesota, everything is about muskies," he said. "It's not only the topic of all angling conversations, but it's the dominant commercial icon—there are muskie bars, muskie tackle shops, muskie motels—it can't be escaped. Before I started fly fishing, my dad took me on a fishing trip to Wolf Lake, and I caught my first keeper on a Mepps Musky Killer. That night at the lodge, they brought out a cake in the shape of a muskie to commemorate my good luck. An old-timer came over and clapped me on the shoulder and said, 'Son, I've been muskie fishing my whole life; I've never caught a keeper.' I knew then how special muskies were, and that they'd be part of my life.

"After I'd been fly fishing for a while, my thoughts began to drift back toward muskies. I didn't have any preconceived notions about what was possible with a fly rod. I soon made the connection that if you could catch tarpon or trout on a fly, you could probably catch a muskie. I figured if the fish are so hard to catch any way— they've been dubbed the fish of ten thousand casts—it wouldn't be a big deal to try with a fly. If I struck out, my efforts would be on par with the results most of the conventional gear guys were seeing. The first time I ever went muskie fishing with my fly rod, I got a small but legally sized fish. Once you see the ferocity and grace of a large muskie annihilating your fly, you're changed. It's one of the great takes in a world of great takes. They're such terrifyingly effective predators. I've watched fishing buddies react when a muskie is about to eat their fly—they scream, they try to get to the back of the boat, they want to move away; it's like someone pulled a gun on you."

Still, the grabs are not frequent. "I like to compare fly fishing for muskie with climbing a mountain—it's an attainable but difficult goal," Robert added. "You need to maintain a cautious optimism that a fish is going to present itself, even though you've been casting for eight hours and haven't seen a thing. You have to imagine that it's going to happen, have a positive visualization of you hooking, fighting, and landing—and, of course, releasing a muskie. These are moody creatures and seem to know—and strike—the moment you drop your guard. Not everyone can handle that.

"For me, chasing muskie with a fly rod is a summation of why I love fly fishing. It's the challenge of learning to understand a difficult-to-catch fish and then applying a new approach to making it happen. Sometimes they put me in my place and remind me that I can't ever learn it all. That aspect alone keeps me coming back. But when they take, I always experience a child-like intensity and sense of awe. It's the thrill that never stops giving. Every fish is like the first one."

ABOUT THE ANGLER

ROBERT TOMES has worked as a guide in Alaska and regularly travels to fish New Zealand, South America, Canada, the Bahamas, and other fishing destinations. He is a regional editor of *Fly Fish America* magazine and is the author of numerous fly-fishing articles for *Fish & Fly, Fly Rod & Reel, Ten & Two Magazine,* and *MidCurrent.* Robert is the author of *Muskie on the Fly* (www.muskieontheflybook.com), the definitive book on the topic, and is the holder of several line-class muskie world records.

DONALD TRUMP JR.

An antidote to work

IT MAY BE A BIT OF A STRETCH TO PICTURE DONALD TRUMP SR. on a river—unless it's one that happens to pass through one of his championship golf courses. But for Donald Jr., it's a whole different story. "The outdoors is my church," he began. "Being in nature gives me a great perspective on everything, on how you fit in to the larger picture. A day on the river lets me recharge my batteries. It's cathartic; it helps me decompress from the rigors of working in a demanding field for a demanding boss. Fly fishing gives me something to look forward to during the week."

Like so many boys and girls, Donald was introduced to fishing by one of his grandfathers. "My grandfather Milos was from Czechoslovakia," he continued, "and he'd come over to New York a few times a year to visit. He was a blue-collar guy, and I think he saw that the lifestyle we had was very urban. He wanted my siblings and me to experience something beyond what he perceived as a city life around spoiled rich kids. He introduced us to archery, motocross, and fishing to give us a taste of a different sort of life. In that same spirit, he started taking me back to the Czech Republic with him. On these trips, I realized that there was another side to life, and that I shouldn't take things for granted. I also got really hooked on the outdoors.

"When I was twelve, my grandpa passed away, and my parents were going through tough times. I was sent to a boarding school that year in Pennsylvania, and I had one teacher who was a wing shooter, one that was a fly fisher. They took me under their wings, and my interest in those pursuits took off. My interest in the outdoors helped me avoid a lot of trouble I could've gotten into. This continued into college. When I was at University of Pennsylvania, while my fellow students were recovering from hangovers on Saturday morning, I'd head off to go fishing in Carlisle (Pennsylvania) or deer hunting in New York." After graduation, Donald headed west to Colorado. "I may be the first Wharton grad to leave school and become a ski and trout bum," he quipped. "During the spring and summer, I'd work for a few months, and then spend a month living from the back of my truck, hitting all the blue-ribbon rivers in Colorado, Wyoming, and Montana. It's amazing how much fishing you can get in with the energy of a twenty-one year old."

Although those carefree days of fishing his way across the great rivers of the West are in the past, Donald still finds many opportunities to wet a line. "As the seasons change, my fishing focus changes," he said. "In the spring, I love to fish the challenging rivers of the Delaware system—the Willowemoc, the Beaverkill, and East and West Branches of the Delaware itself. (Donald has a cabin on the East Branch, roughly two and a half hours from Manhattan.) The fishing here can be very technical. The trout are finicky, keying in on one very specific stage of each hatch. I love that cat-and-mouse game. In the summer I enjoy getting out on Long Island Sound to chase stripers and blues. I try to get to the Salmon River in Pulaski, New York, in the fall to fish for the steelhead and big migratory browns that come into the system to spawn. In the winter, I try to find a chance to head south and fish the salt. I love the tug of a striped marlin. I may be a better saltwater angler than a trout fisherman, as I have a pretty long cast. At the end of the day, I love it all. None of it's the same, yet all of it's the same. I have a good deal of travel in my job. If there's a chance to fish or hunt where I'm going, I'll travel with a rod or a gun if there's time to get a little outdoor activity in."

Donald is fortunate to have found a partner who is very understanding of his passions—so understanding that she was willing to give him leave to fish on three out of the five days of their honeymoon! "We were in Cabo San Lucas, Mexico, and I was fishing with Grant Hartman (of Baja Anglers)," he recalled. "We motored way offshore and hit a pod of striped marlin. There were bait balls the size of VWs, and the marlin were slashing through the bait like bluefish. This went on for nine hours. Grant said that in thirty years of fishing in the region, he'd never seen anything like this. Casting a fly into that amount of bait, it was difficult to get the marlin to take, but still we caught enough. I had a cutoff time for the day's fishing; it wouldn't set a good precedent with my wife Vanessa to be late, even though it was the greatest fishing I'd ever seen. We had a few minutes left and I cast into the melee when suddenly the marlin bolted in all directions and a shadow appeared out of nowhere. A humpback whale breached thirty feet from the boat and swallowed the entire bait ball—including my fly! As you'd imagine, the line was screaming off my reel. All I could think was that I was going to be late getting back because I'd hooked a whale. Eventually I popped it off. Grant commented that that humpback was probably the largest animal ever hooked on a fly rod!"

Whether it's chasing striped marlin (or humpbacks) in Baja or tying flies at home on evenings during the week, Donald maintains that fly fishing is an important part of his life. "Fly fishing has taught me the importance of patience and perseverance," he continued. "It's also helped me recognize that there's more to life than work. I may have to occasionally check my BlackBerry while I'm floating down the river, but I still realize that work is not the end-all. It's not always catching the big steelhead or marlin that makes the experience special. Sometimes it's getting the six-inch dink on the day's last cast when you thought you were going to get skunked that really stands out.

"I'm adamant that my kids get a taste of fishing. You can't force them, though. We have a little pond on our property in Connecticut. I'll take my kids down there sometimes to fish. We'll catch two or three sunfish on worms in fifteen or twenty minutes, and then we'll head home. My thinking is that if I give them a little and then pull back, they'll want more on their own."

ABOUT THE ANGLER

DONALD TRUMP JR. is an executive vice president at the Trump Organization and directs new project acquisition and development for the company throughout the world. He also actively oversees the Trump Organization's current and new property portfolio, which contains more than seventy projects. He is involved in all aspects of real estate development, from deal evaluation, analysis, and predevelopment planning to construction, branding, marketing, operations, sales, and leasing. In addition to his real estate interests, Donald Jr. is an accomplished and sought-after speaker. He has spoken extensively throughout the United States and has given keynote speeches internationally, notably in Dubai and India. He has also been featured as an advisor on the highly acclaimed NBC show *The Apprentice*, and is now a star of the *Celebrity Apprentice*, currently approaching its third season. An avid philanthropist, Donald Jr. sits on the board of directors of Operation Smile and is strongly involved in the Eric Trump Foundation.

APRIL VOKEY

*A respite from chaos,
a quest for survival*

APRIL VOKEY STILL RECALLS WHEN SHE REALIZED that fly fishing was her destiny—though the details are a little fuzzy. "My dad remembers the day in question better than I do," April began, "but the way he tells the story goes like this: I was seventeen or eighteen and came home from gear fishing on the Chilliwack River (outside of Vancouver, Canada) with the stupidest gaze on my face. 'I've seen the most incredible thing today,' I said. 'I saw a man fly fishing in the river. It was the most elegant thing I've ever seen. I have to figure out a way to do this, and figure out a way to make a living at it.'"

It took several years and much perseverance. But today, April is a frequent guest on fly-fishing TV programs and a respected guide on the Dean River and other fisheries around British Columbia.

"I had started fishing with dedication when I was sixteen, using bait and spoons for salmon," April explained. "I fished to get away from the chaos of the rough neighborhood where I grew up. I always fished alone; I think it was something I did to underscore my independence. Angling by myself gave me the confidence to feel comfortable in potentially dangerous situations. Fishing was also something I did to become one with myself. I connect it with the idea of survival, the notion that I'm stalking fish, hunting fish. Humans have been hunting and fishing to survive since time immemorial. Fishing gets me close to the very basic reason for what I'm on

LEFT
British Columbia's Dean River, one of April Vokey's favorite places to pursue steelhead.

the planet for—to survive. Though I don't need to catch or even hook a fish to get a thrill. Finding the fish is enough."

Most of April's guiding business has been built around British Columbia's totem sport fish, steelhead. She shared how she first came to chase these oceangoing rainbow trout. "I had been fishing for a year on the Chilliwack for all five of the Pacific salmon species with spinning gear, and I found them pretty easy to catch. One day I met an old bait fisherman on the river, Dave Puffer, and he asked me to fish with him. I declined, as I always fished alone. He asked me several times, and eventually I agreed. I took my younger sister out to the river with me so I wouldn't be alone with Dave (in case he had nonangling motives), and my parents watched us from the parking lot near the river. Dave, it turned out, was a fantastic guy, and we became friends. He would tell me stories about the other sea-run fish that came into the river, the steelhead, and how hard they were to catch. It got into my head; being told I couldn't have steelhead made me want them that much more. When I finally began catching them, they seemed wild and mean—somewhat like me at the time! I caught them on roe at first, and then I fished a spoon. The more I learned about fly fishing for steelhead, the more I came to understand that swinging flies was a lot like working a spoon. At the same time, I began to realize that I'd been born in a place that offers the best steelhead fishing in the world. It seemed meant to be that I'd one day be a steelhead guide.

"In those early days, I was completely obsessed," April continued. "When I turned twenty-one, I started cocktailing at a nearby casino. I'd waitress all night—from 8:30 p.m. until 4:30 a.m.—go home and sleep two or three hours or take a quick snooze in my car while waiting for the sun to rise and then fish all day. I'd still have makeup on and even sported fake nails, which was encouraged by casino food and beverage management to ensure that our hands were presentable while handling poker chips. Some of the anglers I'd see in the parking lot or on the water would chuckle in thinking that I was getting fancied up to go fishing! The joke was on them...I simply didn't have the time to take it off. That was good time that could be spent fishing! The looks and whispers didn't matter; I knew that to be taken seriously on the river, I'd have to really know what I was doing. So I did my best to spend upward of three hundred days a year on the water to get the experience. I think my parents thought I was wasting my life. 'What are you doing all day?' they'd ask. 'I'm doing research,' I'd reply. This was true, as I'd started Fly Gal Ventures (April's guiding company) at the age of twenty-three and was determined to pursue it as a part-time venture."

Although more and more women have taken up guiding, the fairer sex still represents a minority in the guiding ranks. Some less open-minded or more chauvinistic sports may be dismissive of female guides, especially in pursuit of steelhead. But April has found a positive client-guide experience to be more a function of expectations than gender. "When I began guiding, I was working for someone else," she explained, "and he'd promise his clients the world. When we'd get out on the river, I'd have to break the news that winter steelhead fishing is hard, and we might only get a fish every few days. I left the other guide service and started Fly Gal soon after. With my own company, I can set expectations properly: If you want to use conventional gear, you'll probably get a fish; if you want to fish with flies, it's going to be tougher. I like to think that going out with a female guide, the client's angling experience is something more than a testosterone-packed battle that's defined by landing a fish. I'm not intimidating, and I want clients to know that I'm not there on the bank to judge them, just there to help them understand the fishery a bit more and to share the day. After all, most people say that having a hot lunch on the river and swapping fish stories is a big part of the experience."

At the tender age of twenty-five, April was involved in an accident that put her life—and the importance of fly fishing in her life—into sharp focus. "I was towing a boat up to Williams Lake with a friend, and a drunk driver crossed over the dividing line and slammed into my truck head-on. Both vehicles were going sixty miles per hour; the other driver's three-quarter-ton truck came through the front, my boat came through the back. My right foot was completely shattered, every bone and joint crushed. The doctors rebuilt the foot as best as they could, but the prognosis was grim: 'You won't be able to stand up longer than an hour,' they said. 'You won't fish or hike again.' After I was released from the hospital, I made it two weeks before I thought I was going to go crazy. I called my physical therapist and said, 'I can't stay inside any longer. Can I go fishing?' 'What kind of fishing?' the P.T. questioned back. 'Lake fishing in a pram.' I got a tentative okay, and some friends drove me over to a local lake and loaded me in the pram. I fished for twenty-eight consecutive days. The rowing helped me stay in shape, and the fishing kept me positive.

"At the time of the accident, I was still waitressing at night. The accident—and my convalescence—changed me forever. It made me realize that life was short, that I had to appreciate every single day…and to do that, I'd need to dedicate myself to something I love."

April quit her waitressing job and began devoting herself to fly fishing and guiding full-time. Only British Columbia's steelhead are unhappy about that decision.

ABOUT THE ANGLER

APRIL VOKEY lives in British Columbia, Canada, and is a conservation-minded steelhead, salmon, and trout guide. She is a Federation of Fly Fishers Certified Casting Instructor, a fly-fishing columnist, Patagonia ambassador, and a lead angler for Fly Max Films. She can be found at www.flygal.ca or through her popular fundraiser, Flies for Fins (www.flies4fins.com).

JAMES & JAMIE WILLIAMSON

Getting to hang out with my son/my dad

ON STAGE WITH IGGY AND THE STOOGES, Rock and Roll Hall of Famer James Williamson's guitar style has been called "how you would imagine Darth Vader to sound if he was in a band." On the river much of that intensity is given over to trying to keep up with his son, Jamie. "Both Jamie and I are pretty competitive people," James began. "It became apparent early on that Jamie was catching most of the fish, though I was trying much harder. He's an avid angler who catches fish; I'm an avid angler trying to keep up with my son!"

James and Jamie's fly-fishing partnership began many years ago in Wyoming. "When Jamie was about thirteen, we started going to a dude ranch, the HF Bar in Saddlestring (near the Bighorn National Forest) for an annual vacation," James continued. "There's a lovely little creek—Rock Creek—running through the property. The cook at the ranch gave us our first lessons. We went back to the HF Bar for a number of years. Fishing wasn't our only focus, but we got out on Rock Creek each visit and became more and more proficient. The ranch isn't too far from the Bighorn in Montana, and one year we decided to branch out and try our luck up north. We fished with guides there and began learning more and more about fly fishing. The fish were bigger and fought harder. I think we both got taken with the sport then. When we got home, we got involved with a local fly-fishing club, Flycasters Inc. of San Jose. We improved our casting and I got into fly tying."

LEFT
Introducing a son or daughter to fly fishing can be as satisfying as landing the fish of a lifetime.

"For a while most of our fishing was on the Bighorn," Jamie chimed in. "The next turning point came when my dad got a two-month sabbatical (from Advanced Micro Devices, where James Sr. was an executive, having taken what would turn out to be a thirty-plus-year sabbatical from rock 'n' roll). We fished for most of that time, doing a tour of the West's blue-ribbon trout fisheries. We fished the Big Hole, the Beaverhead and DePuy's in Montana, the Green River in Utah, the Henry's Fork in Idaho, the San Juan in New Mexico, among many others. This cemented our obsession."

"One of my proudest fly-fishing moments came on that sabbatical trip," James added. "We were in a motel room in a town near the Henry's Fork. I was busy tying up some caddis patterns for the next day. Jamie looked at what I'd tied and said 'Those things will never work.' I tied one on the next morning, made a few casts, and had a fish on right away. Pretty soon Jamie was asking for one of the flies. We caught fish with them all day."

As the fishing bug burrowed deeper into Jamie's existence, the annual trips with dad to Montana or Idaho became insufficient. "I was in high school at the time and began looking for ways to fish more frequently," Jamie explained. "There were some little creeks in the hills outside San Jose that I could fish, but I started to learn about the opportunities in the Redding, California, area. I read articles about the great rainbow fishing on the lower Sacramento and the other rivers there, and dad planned a trip."

James picked up the story. "We ended up staying at Clearwater Lodge (on the banks of the Pit River), and Dick Galland (then owner) booked us a float trip," he said. "The guide we went out with was not very experienced. We got in trouble in some rapids; the boat flipped. It was December, and we had to swim in our waders. It was pretty scary, but we survived…and we didn't give up on fishing. In fact, these days most of our fly fishing is in California, up on the Trinity River, hunting steelhead."

Jamie's time as an undergraduate in Washington helped foster an interest in the at-times inscrutable sea-run rainbows. "I attended Whitman College in Walla Walla, and there were streams everywhere," he recalled. "Many of the Snake River tributaries had runs of steelhead, and we'd find some huge fish. Occasionally, a hatchery fish would make it back to campus for the barbecue. If the steelhead weren't present, some of the rivers had trout. Fishing was a great way to take my mind off my studies and I had some good friends to share the experience with. I brought home some pictures and told dad about the action, and I think it piqued his interest."

"Our first time out on the Trinity, the fishing didn't go very well," James recounted. "It was cold and dreary; we weren't finding any fish. I found myself thinking, 'Why are we doing this?' A few outings later I caught one, and we thought we had done pretty well with one fish between us. We mentioned this to one of the guides at The Fly Shop in Redding, Ernie Denison. He said that fourteen-fish days aren't out of the realm of possibility on the Trinity. That raised an eyebrow. We started to do better out there. The Trinity's steelhead aren't enormous as steelhead go, but they're about as much as I can handle. After you catch some steelhead, it's pretty hard to go back to trout. With our schedules as they are these days, Jamie and me are not able to log as many days together on the water as we'd like. But we still make it a point to do a winter steelheading trip on the Trinity each year."

Has the competitive gap closed at all over the years? Yes and no. "The fact is, Jamie outfishes me five or ten to one on any given trip," James conceded. "You can put him in a bucket of crap, and he'll find a fish there. I've stopped being competitive; it's not in my best self-interest!" "I've managed to log more time on the water than my dad," Jamie said graciously, "and have been able to pick up some pretty good techniques from the great guides we've fished with."

There may not be many occasions when the worlds of proto-punk hard rock and fly fishing collide. But James did describe one such incident that occurred in 2011.

"The Stooges had been scheduled to play a few gigs in San Francisco at the Warfield Theater in September, but Iggy had fractured his foot and we had to postpone the shows. We were slated to make them up in early December. Just before the gigs, Jamie and I went out fishing with one of our regular guides, Lonnie Boles. Lonnie lives in Corning (south of Redding); he's kind of a country guy; I certainly couldn't picture him as having been a big Stooges fan. When we finished up fishing, I invited him to come down to the show. I honestly didn't think he'd come; it's a long ride from Corning to San Francisco, and our music didn't seem to be his style. But it was a sincere gesture. Much to my surprise, he came down and brought his wife. Seeing Lonnie there at a Stooges show was a surreal experience. But he and his wife seemed to dig it."

ABOUT THE ANGLERS

JAMES WILLIAMSON appeared on the music scene in 1970s as a guitarist with the influential band the Stooges, fronted by Iggy Pop. After cowriting songs with Iggy and playing on several seminal rock albums—including *Raw Power* and *Kill City*—James left the music business. After earning an electrical engineering degree from California Polytechnic State University, he went on to a successful career in the electronics industry, including ten years as vice president of technology standards for Sony. In 2009, James rejoined the Stooges; his first gig with the band in thirty-five years was for forty thousand fans in Sao Paolo, Brazil! In March 2010, the Stooges were inducted into the Rock and Roll Hall of Fame.

JAMIE WILLIAMSON was born in Claremont, California, in 1981. A nature enthusiast and avid fly fisher, Jamie spent much of his childhood and adolescence outdoors. Over the course of his education, his love for the outdoors manifested itself in a passion for the biological sciences. In 2000, Jamie was admitted to Whitman College, where he majored in biology and environmental science. He graduated in 2004 with an interest in scientific and risk communication, which he studied in a master's program at Cornell University. At the culmination of his degree, Jamie returned to the West Coast to apply his knowledge of the life sciences and communication in a career as a medical writer in the biotechnology industry.

HENRY WINKLER

It's a washing machine for your brain

"MY HEART LIVES IN NEW YORK, where I was born and raised," Henry Winkler has said. "My body lives in Los Angeles, where I do much of my work. My soul lives in Montana, where I fish. I am most at peace on a river in Montana. I liken the experience to a washing machine for my brain. Being there is transforming. While under the Big Sky, I am only concerned with fishing and catching. If you allow your mind to wander anywhere else, you will neither catch nor land your trout. In Montana, I'm so focused on fishing that my mind is cleared of everything else. Catching trout is on my brain from the time I break out my rod and reel and start practicing my casts in the driveway at home until I leave Montana at the end of each trip.

"Fly fishing has helped me reconnect to all that is around me by putting me back in touch with the natural world, which feeds my own natural instincts. To survive in large cities, sometimes you have to tune out all the noise and chaos around you. On the river though, I tune in once again to all five senses, as well as to my gut instincts. You have to pay attention to all that you hear, see, touch, taste, and smell in the wilderness, and you have to act on your intuition if you are going to catch any fish."

LEFT
Casting from a driftboat is the best way to cover the big rivers in western Montana.

Like so many anglers, Henry got his start with the help of a friend; though many of us may not have had our first casting lesson in a Beverly Hills pool. "My lawyer, Skip Brittenham III, and his best friend, the late literary agent Leonard Hanzer, invited my wife Stacey and me to join them on a fishing trip down the Smith River in Montana, circa 1993," Henry recalled. "We were excited by the idea but intimidated too, as both Skip and Leonard were serious fly fishers. Neither Stacey nor I had ever cast a line. The only trout we'd seen were those we'd ordered as entrées, usually with side salads. Fortunately, before Skip took two Hollywood greenhorns into the wilds of Montana, he gave us a few lessons in his Beverly Hills backyard. We practiced our first casts into the crystal-clear waters of his swimming pool. Skip told me that hand-eye coordination was a big factor in fly fishing. 'Whoops! Count me out!' I thought. I had undiagnosed dyslexia as a child, and as a result spent most of my childhood with my self-esteem around my ankles. Along with my learning disability, I had trouble with hand-eye coordination. Whatever the playground sport, I was usually among the last picked—if I was picked at all."

Henry has obviously overcome these obstacles, in life and on the river. "When I speak to young people," he continued, "one of the things I tell them is that the anticipatory fear of trying something is always far worse than actually doing it. With fly fishing, it isn't any different. When I was learning to cast, my old fears of failure crept up on me. But in practicing over and over, I discovered casting was not as complicated as I'd envisioned, and that when I broke the cast down into steps, there was a simple elegance to the sport. There's no kidding around when I describe my technique as U-G-L-Y. I don't have the precision or the economy of movement you see with the most graceful fly-fishing *artistes*. I'm probably at 12:30 and then 4:00 instead of 10:00 and 2:00, but thankfully trout can't tell time."

"People tell me that my work on the *Royal Pains* TV series is some of the most relaxed acting I've ever done," he added. "I believe my comfort in my role as Eddie Lawson has to do with the self-confidence I've gained out on the river. My only regret is that I didn't pick up a rod and reel earlier in life."

The importance of following your instincts—in fishing, as in life—was struck home for Henry on the banks of the Beaverhead one dusk fifteen year ago. "I was with my son Max, who was twelve years old at the time, and we were staying at a lodge owned by director and screenwriter David Ondaatje, who is also the owner of the legendary R. L. Winston Rod Company in Twin Bridges. The Beaverhead runs through David's property. One evening Max and I went out for a night hatch. David, a wonderful fishing person himself, served as our guide, which was a good thing because once the sun went down, I couldn't see my own feet. 'Listen for the fish,' David said. Since he is a native of Canada, I thought at first that he was giving me the sort of cryptic stage direction known only to Toronto thespians. Not knowing how else to respond, I did as I was told. I listened, and lo and behold, for the first time in my life, I heard the wondrous sound of fish slurping! They were feeding on the last hatch of bugs for the day.

"'Cast your line where the fish are feeding,' David instructed. My son became my personal cheerleader and coach at that point: 'C'mon, Dad, you can do it! This is great!' Since I always do EXACTLY what my directors, guides, and sons tell me, I cast blindly into the inky trench of the river, toward the fishy slurps. Instantly something took the fly. I could feel it was a good-size fish, and it turned out to be an eighteen-inch brown trout. Ten seconds earlier, I had no idea this fish was even in the same zip code.

"There was not a single beam of moonlight. I caught that lovely trout purely on Winkler sonar. What a wonderful experience that was! What a wonderful feeling. I'd accomplished something rare in the world of sports and certainly rare in the world of me. It's something you never forget.

"Even better I did it with Max cheering on his dad. I'll never forget that moment: the darkness, the sound of the fish feeding on swarming insects, and especially the cheers from my son, which were like echoes of all the encouragement Stacey and I had given him and his brother, Jed, and sister, Zoe, over the years.

"That moment is on my life's highlight reel. I seem to have more of those magical moments in Montana than anywhere else. Being there allows me to be present and to savor all that occurs as it occurs."

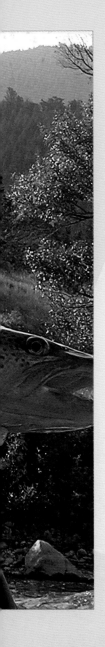

ABOUT THE ANGLER

HENRY WINKLER is an actor, producer, director, and coauthor of seventeen children's novels (with Lin Oliver) in the Hank Zipzer series. He is probably best known for his role as the Fonz on *Happy Days*; he currently appears as Eddie Lawson on USA Channel's *Royal Pains*. In 2011, he published *I've Never Met an Idiot on the River: Reflections on Family, Photography and Fly-Fishing*. Henry lives in Los Angeles with his wife Stacey, two dogs, and five fly-fishing rods. They fish primarily in Idaho and Montana.

CHRIS WOOD

Maintaining a sense of optimism

IT WAS AN EFFORT TO REACH OUT TO A CHILD and a fishing trip that involved
no fishing that led Chris Wood to a career in conservation.

"I was part of the Big Brothers Big Sisters program at Middlebury College in
Vermont," Chris began. "Students are matched with kids in the community who
might benefit from mentorship. My "little brother" was hyperactive. He seemed to
calm down a bit when he was in a natural setting. I had taken him spin fishing a few
times for perch. His parents thought that fly fishing might be good for him, and they
got him a rod. I had the Orvis Green Mountain seven-weight that my parents had
given me as a gift, and we headed out. We didn't fish all that much, but David would
be much more relaxed by the water. Not long after we began our fly-fishing adventures, his family moved away. I still had the fly rod, so I began fishing on my own.
There are a number of decent trout streams around Middlebury, and suffice it to say,
I did not have perfect attendance for my morning classes. For a time, my bank card
code was "0523" for the vital statistics of a rainbow I caught out of Otter Creek at the
Middlebury Falls (five pounds, twenty-three inches).

"I did graduate, and like many good liberal-arts grads, I began applying my degree—
by bartending, working in an ice cream factory, and coaching high school football
at home in New Jersey. Near the end of the summer I got a letter from a Middlebury
friend, Mick Kelly, who was living in a tent on the Homer Spit in Alaska and

bartending at a place called Land's End. He encouraged me to come out and fish for salmon, and I went. During an evening at the rougher bar in Homer that involved a libation called the bar mat, Mick encouraged me to take his car and go down to the Kenai Peninsula and fish the Anchor River where it runs into the salt for silver salmon. Thanks to the bar mats, I didn't get a particularly early start the next day, and by the time I reached the mouth of the Anchor, it was getting dark. I pitched a tent and went to sleep…and woke up with water lapping at the entrance flap. Mick's car was parked between the tent and the water. I hadn't counted on the big Alaskan tides; back in New Jersey, the tides are eighteen inches. It took most of the next day to dry the car out; I must have used three cans of Gumout. To this day, Mick doesn't know his car was underwater. (At least until now.)

"By late afternoon, I was ready to go fishing. I had my seven-weight, a pair of brand-new rubber Ranger bootfoot waders, and a handful of flies. As I walked up the bank, I looked down into the river and saw these gigantic fish, much larger than any I'd ever seen. On closer inspection, they had these grotesque hooked jaws, and their bodies were covered in gnarly sores. Being a Jersey kid, I concluded that there had been a terrible industrial accident. A train must have fallen off a trestle and dumped chemicals into the Anchor, disfiguring all the fish! I continued upriver, being careful to avoid what must have been acid-laced water. I came upon a guy who was wading into the river with a rod. 'What are you doing?' I called out, hoping to alert him to the chemical disaster. He looked at me like I was crazy and said 'I'm fishing.' 'What happened to the fish?' I called back. 'They're salmon,' he replied shaking his head and returning to his angling. I walked back to Mick's car, took off my waders, drove into town, and took out a book on salmon from the local library. I read it by my campfire (which I'd moved back from the water). I understood now what I'd seen, and I was fascinated. I wanted to somehow be part of this. I went back to Homer without ever fishing. Before returning home I wrote the ice cream factory a letter of resignation…not realizing that ice cream factory workers didn't have to write letters of resignation.

"When I got back home, I went to the ice cream factory and resigned face to face. That very morning, I happened to see a photo in the paper of a biologist named Keith Edwards, out in Idaho. The story concerned a sockeye salmon that had been dubbed 'Lonesome Larry.' It was the only fish that had returned from the Pacific to Redfish Lake (near Stanley). The caption had a quote from the biologist that read something like 'It saddens me to say I work at a lake named for a fish that doesn't live here anymore.' Lonesome Larry had swum eight hundred miles inland, gaining eight thousand feet in elevation while traversing eight dams. I decided then and there that I wanted to work to help save the salmon, these wonderful fish that bring nutrients from the Pacific to the mountains to sustain the web of life.

"There's a great quote from Aldo Leopold (from *Round River*) that nicely sums up the uncomfortable position that many conservationists find themselves in:

> One of the penalties of an ecological education is that one lives alone in a world of wounds. Much of the damage inflicted on land is quite invisible to laymen. An ecologist must either harden his shell and make believe that the consequences of science are none of his business, or he must be the doctor who sees the marks of death in a community that believes itself well and does not want to be told otherwise.

People working in the conservation profession today are constantly dealing with loss that others may not see. Exhibit One—practically every endemic trout in the West is proposed for protection under the Endangered Species Act. Yet, we maintain a sense of optimism. For us, it's not about administering the decline of a species or ecosystem, but about seeing the potential for recovery. I think this speaks to who fly fishers are as a breed. You have to be an optimist to take a bit of fur and feather and wire, cast it at river ghosts, and expect them to materialize on the end of your line. There's not a single fly angler I've encountered who doesn't believe that on the last cast of a long day that they're going to hook the best fish of their life.

"I suppose that's why the average Trout Unlimited chapter donates two thousand hours of habitat work. We know we can make a difference."

On a more recent trip to Alaska, Chris had the chance to do a little fishing. "I was visiting my friend Brian Kraft's Alaska Sportsman's Lodge in the fall of 2011 on the Kvichak, one of the eight rivers that flow into Bristol Bay," he recalled. "There are two mining companies that have proposed development of the largest open-pit mine in the world above the headwaters of the Kvichak. The proposed mine's acid-laden tailings would be held back by a seven-hundred-foot earthen dam—this in a very seismically active area. The Bristol Bay region is one of the most fecund areas in the world for wild Pacific salmon. Should the earthen dam collapse, it would be disastrous for the fishery. Thus far efforts to develop the Pebble Mine have been defeated, but it's an ongoing battle.

"I didn't have much time to fish on this trip, but I did get out in front of the lodge one afternoon. I was fishing flesh flies; the river's huge rainbows (which can reach thirty inches) feed on decaying salmon in the fall. Sometimes they don't wait until the salmon are dead to grab bits of flesh. I found a nice hole at the bottom of a gravel bar and let my fly drift through. Sure enough, I saw the line move and set the hook. Twenty-five yards away, a fish came four feet out of the water. 'What's that fish doing?' I wondered…and then I realized it was on the end of my line. When I got it to hand, it was only twenty-four inches. Not my longest fish, but my strongest. That fish is a great example of what can happen if anglers understand and support the connection between sound habitat and remarkable fisheries."

ABOUT THE ANGLER

CHRIS WOOD is the president and chief executive officer of Trout Unlimited. Before taking on this role, he ran TU's conservation programs. Prior to coming to Trout Unlimited in September 2001, Chris worked for the chief of the U.S. Forest Service and was an architect of a policy that protects fifty-eight million acres of public land from development. Chris began his career as a temporary employee with Forest Service Research in Idaho and also worked for the Bureau of Land Management. He is the author and coauthor of two books, including *Watershed Restoration: Principles and Practices* (AFS 1997) and *From Conquest to Conservation: Our Public Land Legacy* (Island Press, 1997). A graduate of Middlebury College, Chris lives in Washington, D.C., with his wife, Betsy, and three sons, Wylie, Casey, and Henry Trace.

PHOTO CREDITS

Pages 2, 38, 56, 62, 140, 152, and 159: photographs © Jim Klug/klugphotos.com; page 8: photograph © Paul Sharman/paulsharmanoutdoors.com; page 13: photograph courtesy of Conway Bowman; page 14: photograph © Lisa Cutter; page 19: photograph © Ralph Cutter; page 20: photograph © Tim Romano/timromano.com; page 24: photograph courtesy of Kirk Deeter; page 26: photograph © Russ Schnitzer/schnitzerphoto.com; page 31: photograph courtesy of Michael B. Enzi; page 32: photograph © Bob Linsenman; page 37: photograph courtesy of Bill Ford, Jr.; page 43: photograph courtesy of John Gierach; pages 44, 50, 68, 80–81, 85, 92, 110, 116–17, and 146: photographs © Brian O'Keefe; page 49: photograph courtesy of Carl Hiaasen; page 55: photograph © J. Nichols; page 61: photograph courtesy of Craig Mathews; page 67: photograph courtesy of Mac McKeever; page 73: photograph courtesy of Frank Moore; page 74: photograph © Steven Bly; page 79: photograph courtesy of Ed Nicholson; page 86, 98, and 128: photographs © Tosh Brown/toshbrown.com; page 90: photograph courtesy of Flip Parrot; page 97: photograph courtesy of Nick Price; page 103: photograph courtesy of Tom Rosenbauer; pages 104 and 134: photographs © Ken Morrish; page 109: photograph courtesy of Dave Rosgen; page 145: photograph courtesy of Robert E. Rubin; page 120: photograph courtesy of Robert Swan; page 122: photograph © Walter Hodges; page 127: photograph courtesy of Robert Tomes; page 132: photograph courtesy of Donald Trump Jr.; page 139: photograph courtesy of April Vokey; page 145: photograph courtesy of James and Jamie Williamson; page 150: photograph courtesy of Henry Winkler; page 157: photograph courtesy of Chris Wood.

Published in 2013 by Stewart, Tabori & Chang
An imprint of ABRAMS

Text copyright © 2013 Chris Santella
Photo credits appear on page 158.

Cataloging-in-Publication Data has been applied for and
can be obtained from the Library of Congress.

ISBN: 978-1-61769-024-2

EDITOR: Jennifer Levesque
DESIGNER: Henk Van Assen (with Loide Marwanga
and Marcela de la Vega)
PRODUCTION MANAGER: Tina Cameron

The text of this book was composed in Quadraat and
Quadraat Sans.

Printed and bound in China

10 9 8 7 6 5 4 3 2 1

Stewart, Tabori & Chang books are available at special
discounts when purchased in quantity for premiums
and promotions as well as fundraising or educational use.
Special editions can also be created to specification.
For details, contact specialsales@abramsbooks.com or
the address below.

ABRAMS
THE ART OF BOOKS SINCE 1949

115 West 18th Street
New York, NY 10011
www.abramsbooks.com